The KING'S DAUGHTER WORKBOOK

Becoming a Woman of God

A Personal Interactive Journey
And a Curriculum for Women's Groups

DIANA HAGEE

Author of *The King's Daughter*

Published by Thomas Nelson Publishers, a Division of Thomas Nelson, Inc., P.O. Box 141000, Nashville, Tennessee, 37214.

Library of Congress Cataloging-in-Publication Data is available.

ISBN 1-4185-0553-6

Printed in the United States of America

05 06 07 08 09—5 4 3 2 1

I dedicate this work to all the women who have taken the Becoming a Woman of God class at Cornerstone Church and around the globe. Their passionate desire to want more of God inspired *The King's Daughter* and now *The King's Daughter Workbook*. I bless you in the Name of the Lord.

"For this reason, ever since I heard about your faith in the Lord Jesus and your love for all the saints, I have not stopped giving thanks for you, remembering you in my prayers. I keep asking that the God of our Lord Jesus Christ, the glorious Father, may give you the Spirit of wisdom and revelation, so that you may know Him better. I pray also that the eyes of your heart may be enlightened in order that you may know the hope to which He has called you, the riches of His glorious inheritance in the saints, and His incomparably great power for us who believe."

— EPHESIANS 2:15-19

ACKNOWLEDGMENTS

To my King who has guided my path during this extraordinary journey;

To my precious husband, John Hagee, who has encouraged the women of our church to be all they can be in Christ;

To Kathy Rudkin and my precious daughter Christina Ketterling, two Women of God whose creativity birthed our King's Daughter Multi-media Facilitators' Package to equip women to reach their destiny;

To Janet Thoma and Teresa Weaver who have shared countless hours of time, tears, and laughter with me as this project has come to realization.

I love you all.

CONTENTS

PART TWO: *A Curriculum for Women's Groups*

part one

Your Personal Journey

chapter one

The King's Daughter:

Becoming a Woman of God

"Yet who knows whether you have come to the kingdom for such a time as this?"
—ESTHER 4:14

In 1999 when I stood at the front of our sanctuary at Cornerstone Church and looked out at the three-hundred teenage girls who were attending our first Woman of God class, I was both excited and frightened. This was one of the first times I had conducted a large teaching series, and I knew the Lord was counting on me to make a difference in these young girls' lives.

These classes were inspired by the Book of Esther. As God positioned Esther to become the queen of Persia, the most powerful nation on earth at that time in history, she had to prepare herself. *Why do we not prepare ourselves to follow God's call on our lives,* I wondered. The result of this thought was a class at our church for the young women of thirteen-to-nineteen years of age to equip them to become women of God. I expected twenty-five to fifty young women to register for the class. Instead more than three-hundred girls flooded the registration tables.

One of the older girls who attended this first Woman of God class was Moriah Weaver. This eighteen-year-old says she was blessed to get into a group with girls her own age, from all kinds of backgrounds, and see that the struggles and problems she thought were unique to her were really quite typical. "For the first time I had a support system with people who were of like faith. I found a safe haven where I could be myself and ask the questions I wanted answered."

The next year when I began the first Woman of God class for women of twenty-to-one-hundred years of age I had that same queasy feeling. I wanted these adults to realize God's love for them and who they were as daughters of the King. I asked the Lord, "Help me to minister to these women as Your servant. Help me to show them Your plans for them as Your beloved daughters."

And the Lord answered my prayer. During the five years of these classes the Lord has blessed the women in our church. Approximately 2,500 women have participated in the Woman of God teaching series at Cornerstone Church, some returning the next year to work as facilitators, like Moriah Weaver, others returning each year to relive the experience and hear any new teaching.

Moriah says, "I agree with Mrs. Hagee when she says that this experience reminds her of peeling an onion. Every year a different layer comes off those who take the class, just as you can peel different layers off an onion. You don't realize that you need to deal with another part of who you are until the next session; at that time you are at a different point in your life."

Another woman in the first adult class was Judy Willingham, a single mom with three children— two boys and a girl. She had been a stay-at-home mom for sixteen years and was on child support and welfare to provide the necessities for her and her children. The hopelessness of her life had her so overwhelmed that her doctor had prescribed Prozac®—but that didn't alleviate her depression. "I was down," Judy told me. "I would lie on the floor and whine and whimper and ask, 'Why me, God? What did I do to deserve this? Why? Why? Why?' People would try to encourage me, but I'd just cut them off. I gave every excuse in the world to stay just where I was, down in that dark hole of depression.

"A friend encouraged me to attend the Woman of God class. At first I didn't want to go, but after I went to the first class, I lived for Tuesday night. I sat right on the front row, as close as I could get. The class jumpstarted my life.

"After several sessions Teresa Weaver asked me to help type out the testimonies. 'I know how to type,' I told Teresa, 'but I don't know how to work a computer.'

"Still Teresa decided to give me a chance; she either knew that God would use this situation in my life or she was so desperate she was willing to take any help, no matter how unprofessional.

"And the work proved to be difficult, since the computer didn't act like a typewriter. As I tried to use the word processing system, I would get all jumbled up. I remember asking Teresa, 'How do you go to a new page?' Thankfully she took time out of her many duties to show me.

"Despite my frustration with the word-processing program, I now had a voice inside me that said, 'You know what? You can learn this, just like you can learn to do anything you want to do.'

"I never would have thought that before the Woman of God class, my self-esteem was so low. I believed I was stupid. I didn't have an education. But after you, Diana, told how the Lord helped you overcome low self-esteem, I decided that if God helped you, He would help me. Many nights I would cry at some of your testimony because I could relate to your feelings of inadequacy. You were so honest. And you'd come so far."

Judy's children had a computer so she began to "play" with the word processing system during the day, teaching herself and asking the kids for help when the process seemed impossible to understand. Then she ordered some learning CDs. And finally she got a job. Her life did change dramatically and I'll tell you more about that in Chapter Six.

Another woman who took the class was Dupe Adedeji, a young Nigerian woman who married a Nigerian American and came to the United States when she was only twenty-six years old. She had felt inferior to her peers as a child because her parents hadn't had the money to provide the "extras"—like clothes and vacations abroad—that her friends were afforded. And now that she was in America, everything was so strange and new to her. "I was just so low," she said, "that I could not do anything. After a while I just stopped thinking about my future. Instead I thought, *Whatever happens, happens. . . .* I was so shy I didn't even want to answer the telephone."

Dupe said that when I talked about being a young pastor's wife who couldn't seem to do anything right, she thought, *That's me. If Diana can do this, I can do it, too.* "I was also blessed," she said, "when you told us, 'You're a beautiful woman. You're a daughter of the King. How dare you put yourself down!'"

Dupe attended the Woman of God class in 2000 and then acted as a facilitator for three additional classes. "The first time I facilitated, I thought, *How can I think I can do this? How can I help other women make changes in their lives?* But then I realized that even though I was facilitating I was also there to learn from the other women. We were all supposed to learn together."

Judy and Dupe are just two of the many women whose lives have been changed by the Woman of God sessions. Their testimonies have shown me that the Lord was the one who inspired me to begin these sessions.

We have conducted five Woman of God seminars at Cornerstone Church, and I have been amazed by how our program has extended throughout the United States and even into foreign countries, like Columbia, Honduras, Mexico, Scotland, and Nigeria.

The classes in Nigeria actually grew out of our sessions here in San Antonio. Dupe Adedeji and her husband, Diran, go there once a year to minister to widows, orphans, prostitutes, and the destitute through their Abundance Ministries. In the past Dupe always stood behind her husband, feeling as if she had nothing to contribute. But after attending the Woman of God classes Dupe thought, *A lot of women in Nigeria need to hear this. If I had heard this when I was younger, I would have lived a more fulfilled life. The women over there will be blessed when I tell them, "You are not to be put down. You are a child of God, a daughter of the King."*

Dupe decided to teach the Woman of God curriculum the next time she and her husband visited Nigeria. She told me about her decision and we furnished her with our handouts and other needed supplies.

Once Dupe got to her homeland she realized what a monumental task she was undertaking. There was no way to advertise the class on radio and television, because of a lack of finances. She'd have to rely on word of mouth. And it would be difficult for the women to come to the class since few in Nigeria have cars, especially the women she wanted to reach.

Dupe decided upon a one-day class, since she would only be in Nigeria for one month. She would give the women breakfast so they could come early in the morning and also provide lunch in the afternoon and snacks in the evening. Over the next week she told people she knew through Abundance Ministry about the event.

The first time Dupe conducted the class she admits she was really scared. Even though there were only twenty-five women, she felt as if she were talking to 25,000 since she had never spoken in front of a group before.

While she was talking she kept asking herself, *Do they understand what I am saying? Am I looking stupid or are they really enjoying themselves?*

At the end of that day everyone crowded around her, asking, "Why don't you do this again? Why didn't you tell more women about this?"

Those words confirmed Dupe's intuition that women in Nigeria would benefit from this curriculum so she decided to do the seminar again the next year. That year she rented a hall and about 255 women arrived. The hall was filled. "I was thinking, whoa! What am I doing here?" Dupe told me. "But I did my best, and afterward a lady I'd known for years came up to me, gave me a big hug, and said, 'I'm so proud of you. You did a great job.'"

And the following year Dupe again had about two hundred women. In each of these sessions Dupe used my book, *The King's Daughter*, often reading a paragraph or so as she taught particular topics.

This book was written to the woman who had forgotten—or never accepted—the fact that she is the King's daughter. It was written to the woman who does not realize that the King wants to give her every good and perfect gift, not because she is perfect but because He is good.

Once we have accepted the Lord Jesus Christ as Savior, we are daughters of the King. However, we must claim that position. We must represent Him in every facet of life. The beauty of walking with Him is that it is never too late to claim that position in His heart. We are all King's daughters.

Let's consider the life of a young woman who saved her people from annihilation.

ESTHER'S CALLING

What do we know about Esther? For starters we know that her uncle, Mordecai, was out of the will of God. The Babylonians had probably taken Mordecai captive during the second deportation that left Jerusalem during the reign of Jeconiah. At some time Esther's parents were killed, and Esther became Mordecai's ward.

By the time of the Book of Esther, God had permitted His people to return to their own land; in fact the Babylonian king Cyrus had given a decree to permit them to return, and those who were in the will of God did return to the land of Israel. Mordecai, however, was among the majority of Jews who decided to remain in the land of their captivity.

When you read the Book of Esther, notice that God's name is never mentioned in this book of the Bible. Nor is there a reference to prayer. Even though Mordecai was one of God's people, he was not walking with God at the beginning of this book. He was, in fact, out of God's will.

Could you be out of the will of God right now? If so, the Lord wants you to claim your inheritance.

THE CLAIM TO YOUR INHERITANCE

Ephesians 1:4 says that every woman has a divine destiny that a sovereign God determined from the foundations of the world: "that we should be holy and without blame before Him in love." And in Ephesians 1:17–19, the apostle Paul specifies some of that calling: "that the God of our Lord Jesus Christ, the Father of glory, may give to you the spirit of wisdom and revelation in the knowledge of Him, the eyes of your understanding being enlightened; that you may know what is the hope of His calling, what are the riches of the glory of His inheritance in the saints, and what is the exceeding greatness of His power toward us who believe, according to the working of His mighty power."

Think about your own life. What might be the calling God has given you? Mention that below:

_____

_____

_____

_____

The apostle Paul goes on in Ephesians 2 to say: "For we are His workmanship, created in Christ Jesus for good works, which God prepared beforehand that we should walk in them" (v. 10).

What good works is God calling you to do? Mention those in the space below:

_____

_____

_____

And Paul ends Ephesians 2 with this description of you and me: "Now, therefore, you are no longer strangers and foreigners, but fellow citizens with the saints and members of the household of God" (v. 19).

We are daughters of the King. And He has given us His power, as Paul mentioned in Ephesians 1 where he said that you may know "the riches of the glory of His inheritance in the saints" and "the exceeding greatness of His power toward us who believe, according to the working of His mighty power" (vv. 18–19).

Have you claimed God's power in your life? Think about the magnitude of that power. God's power . . .

- Created heaven and earth,
- Parted the waters of the Red Sea so that the Hebrew slaves could escape from Pharaoh,
- Defeated the Israelites' enemies time and time again,
- Transformed eleven ordinary men into disciples who converted their known world to Christ—and began a religion that is still changing people's lives today.

This is the gift that has been given to us so that we may fulfill our destiny as daughters of the King.

Many of God's daughters have claimed this gift, particularly the young Esther who was called to serve her Lord at a time such as this. And daughters of the King continually grow in their walk with God.

Test yourself against the directions for personal growth that Paul gave to the Thessalonians. In Chapters Four and Five of First Thessalonians he set these standards for living in God's will. Check the areas that are present in your life:

_____ Sanctification: "that you should abstain from sexual immorality" (1 Thess. 4:3).

_____ Brotherly love for others: "you, yourselves are taught by God to love one another" (4:9).

_____ A peaceful spirit: "to lead a quiet life, to mind your own business" (4:11).

_____ An accepting attitude toward those who are outside the faith: "to walk properly toward them" (4:12).

_____ A ministry to others: "to warn those who are unruly, comfort the faint-hearted, uphold the weak, and be patient with all" (5:14).

_____ Integrity: "to see that no one renders evil for evil to anyone, but always pursue what is good both for yourselves and for all" (5:15).

_____ A thankful attitude: "rejoice always" (5:16) and "in everything give thanks" (5:18).

_____ A continual prayer life: "pray without ceasing" (5:17).

_____ A discerning spirit: "test all things; hold fast what is good" (5:21).

_____ A faithful walk: "abstain from every form of evil" (5:22).

If you realize that you may be out of God's will in some of these areas, write a prayer of repentance below, asking God to help you follow His will in the days ahead. When I ask you to write a prayer in this workbook, I'm asking you to pour your heart out on a piece of paper. I want you to talk to Jesus as if He were standing in front of you. Write what you would say to Him in the space on the following page:

Father, I repent before You of those things I have done that have grieved Your Holy Spirit. They are . . .

_____

_____

Even if you are out of His will, God is standing in the shadows of your life, just as He was in the lives of Mordecai and Esther.

In his *Thru the Bible* commentary, J. Vernon McGee calls this book of the Bible, "The Romance of Providence." "Providence," McGee says, "is the means by which God directs all things; both animate and inanimate; seen and unseen; good and evil toward a worthy purpose, which means His will must finally prevail."[1] McGee gives an even shorter definition of providence when he says: "Providence is the way God leads the man who will not be led."[2]

And McGee goes on to illustrate God's providence in this way: "Providence means that the hand of God is in the glove of human events. When God is not at the steering wheel, He is the backseat driver. He is the coach who calls the signals from the bench. Providence is the unseen rudder on the ship of state. God is the pilot at the wheel during the night watch."[3]

The Psalms also make God's providence very clear: "His kingdom rules over all (Ps. 103:19). And the apostle Paul tells us that God "works all things according to the counsel of His will" (Eph. 1:11).

Mordecai might have forgotten God, but God had not forgotten Mordecai or the nation of Israel. God, and God alone, would determine their fate.

Do you believe that God is standing in the shadows of your life, directing the events from behind the scenes? If so, what difference does that make in your attitude toward each day? Write that in the space on the following page:

Dear Jesus, I had no idea you were in the shadows of my life when
I strayed or felt alone. Now that I know this, I will . . .

If you don't believe that God is in control of what happens to you, read back over God's Word in Psalm 103:19 and Ephesians 1:11. And then watch how God led Mordecai and Esther in their journey as you read through this book of the Bible.

THE JOURNEY BEGINS

In this workbook you will make a personal journey to become a King's daughter as you work through interactive exercises to decipher your divine destiny. Each week, for the next twelve weeks, you will work through personal questions and thought-provoking Scriptures that enable you to deepen your walk with God.

We will look at the same topics discussed in *The King's Daughter*. First you will look at God's will for you in the three parts of your nature: your soul, your spirit, and your body and its environment. In the next chapter we will begin with your soul, your emotions and feelings. Too many of us suffer from low self-esteem. In that chapter we will learn about God's impression of us. (Isn't it truer than our own since He is omnipotent and omnipresent?) Then we will consider your spiritual life: your testimony for Christ and your relationship to the Holy Spirit. Finally we will examine your physical nature: your goals, your sexuality, even your finances and hospitality.

Throughout this workbook we will hear the experiences of women who have taken the Woman of God class and the difference these principles have made in their lives. We will also look at the lives of some well-known Christians and work through the teaching of some Christian leaders in particular areas, like sexuality and finances.

In Part Two you will find the King's Daughter curriculum for women's groups. You might want to work through these lessons as you read the pertinent chapters.

Once you begin to live like a King's daughter, you will never be the same again.

"His kingdom rules over all."

—PSALM 103:19

God *"works all things according to the counsel of His will."*

—EPHESIANS 1:11

chapter two

My Value in God's Eyes:

A Lesson in Self-Esteem

"He chose us in Him before the foundation of the world."

–EPHESIANS 1:4

Throughout my life I have seen myself as unattractive and inadequate. I used to think that my lack of self-esteem made me unusual. Now I'm not so sure. I think many women (and many men by the way) suffer from a lack of self-esteem until they recognize their position in the kingdom of God. Certainly Judy Willingham and Dupe Adedeji felt that way, and most of the women do when they first attend the Woman of God sessions. And they are not unusual. Over the years I've come into contact with many women who seemed to be beautiful, who seemed to have it altogether. Yet underneath they lacked true self-esteem. Kim Alexis, at one time the world's most photographed supermodel, is one example.

In high school Kim looked forward to a career as a pharmacist. Once she was accepted into the University of Rhode Island's five-year pharmacy program, she looked around for ways to make extra money. Some people told her, "You're pretty—you ought to try modeling."

So she called several modeling agencies that told her she had to go to modeling school or charm school first. Kim chose charm school. Her experience there was a challenge to her self-esteem. "The first thing they had me do was take a 'before' picture. I remember being very self-conscious and uncomfortable in my little leotard. I didn't know how to stand, how to pose, what to do with my hands—I just felt completely awkward.

"I felt awkward and inferior at charm school—like a fish out of water. I saw the other girls in the school as much more polished and experienced than I was."[1]

One night when Kim was taking her second course at that school a stranger, an odd little man, sat there watching the girls. No one explained why he was there.

Later when Kim was called into the owner's office she found out. The odd little man was a talent scout for a major New York modeling agency. "How would you like to go to New York and work as a model?" he asked Kim.

Kim's answer: No, thank you. She saw modeling as a part-time job to provide extra spending money for college, not as a full-time career.

Yet the next two times the man returned to the charm school, he coaxed her to change her mind.

Finally John Casablancas, the owner of the New York modeling agency, appeared at the charm school—and offered Kim a career as a professional model. He offered her a one-year contract with a guarantee of $500 a month, whether she worked or not. Kim had been making $1.98 an hour as a clerk in a drugstore in Lockport, Illinois, so she finally decided to give professional modeling a try.

That night, as John Casablancas was saying goodbye, he turned to Kim and said, "By the way, Kim, you need to lose fifteen pounds."

She was a big, muscular girl—not the typical thin waif most people associate with modeling. And she was already involved in strenuous exercise.

"To this day," Kim says, "I can hear John Casablancas say, 'By the way, Kim, you need to lose fifteen pounds.' That's been the thorn in my flesh, the hole in my self-esteem, ever since that day."[2]

Kim says, "I look back on those early days of my modeling career, and the one feeling that comes flooding back, as fresh as if it were yesterday, is a feeling of utter insecurity and vulnerability. I felt like a fish out of water when I was at charm school, I felt the same way when I got into the modeling world, and to some extent, I even feel that way today.

"People don't realize that, even after all the magazine covers, ads, fashion shows, television shows, and movies, I still don't see myself as 'Supermodel Kim Alexis.' Inside, I know I'm still just Kim from Lockport—a walking mass of insecurities and vulnerability."[3]

Maybe you have also seen yourself as a walking mass of insecurities and vulnerability. Maybe you still do. I admit that you may not be able to identify with a super model's feelings of low self-esteem, but you probably can identify with me. I'm the teenager who didn't go to the prom in high school and didn't receive a mum from a boyfriend at Homecoming.

After I accepted Jesus Christ as my Savior when I was nineteen years old, my opinions about myself seemed to improve. But as the "honeymoon" period with Jesus passed, I found myself dealing with feelings of low esteem more than ever. Every time I tried to do something for the Lord, Satan would remind me of my weaknesses.

And self-worth has been a struggle throughout my life. My nose is still too big, my teeth still are too crooked, and my chin line is now drooping.

During the Woman of God sessions, I told the women of my struggles and also said that my relationship with Christ has helped me to get over my lack of self-esteem.

"We're going to identify ourselves in Christ, not in a relationship, not with a man, not with children," I told them. "Not with anything else but Christ, because when that happens, we become strong in Him. When that happens, we can identify who we are in Christ, and we become closer to the image He created. Then we can fulfill the destiny He has for us.

"My purpose is to show you the beautiful woman God created," I said. "How many of you see beauty when you look in the mirror?" I asked the women. No one raised her hand, even when I coaxed them by saying, "Now don't be shy. Be honest."

Then I asked, "How many see ugly when you look in the mirror?" Most of the women raised their hands.

"Satan is using this weakness to keep you from God's best for your life," I told the women, "and you, like me, have allowed him to do so."

OUR PERCEPTION—CORRECTED

Psychologists say that we form opinions of ourselves early in our lives. These opinions are often developed by positive or negative experiences, by others' comments about us, or by our perception of ourselves. Our society has given us role models through fashion models, sports figures, and movie stars. Yet much of what we see in magazines and on the screen is only an illusion.

Kim Alexis says, "Contrary to what many people think, models aren't physically perfect. No one is perfect. We all have flaws. We are all aware of features we don't like. Believe me, we models are the first to know our flaws, the first to hide them—and we dwell on them constantly.

"All models have insecurities. Even if we get paid millions of dollars to be photographed, even if people are constantly telling us, 'You're beautiful! You're the best!'—we know our flaws, we're painfully aware of them, and we are horribly insecure about them. There's not a model in the business who doesn't feel that way—not one. We all wake up every morning, look in the mirror, wince at that flaw, that thorn in our flesh."[4]

The pictures of perfection we see in the magazines and on the screen are not really true, Kim Alexis says. Yet we try to attain this illusion because we look at ourselves through the eyes of a very secular society, not the eyes of a loving Creator.

Unfortunately we are on the path of self-destruction. Satan is not in our lives just to give us a bad day; the Bible says he has come "to steal, and to kill, and to destroy" (John 10:10). He will steal what God has already provided for us free of charge. He will kill any form of hope that lies within our spirits.

The apostle Paul told the early Christians to fight against Satan: "I, therefore, the prisoner of the Lord, beseech you to walk worthy of the calling with which you were called, with all lowliness and gentleness" (Eph. 4:1–2).

Lowliness of mind means that we accept all things that God says about us without argument. Let's examine our portrait in the Word of God as daughters of the King. Write each of these passages of Scripture in the space below. Then apply them to your life.

1. Isaiah 43:4

_____

_____

_____

This Scripture shows me that I am _____.

Therefore I have great value. The Creator of the universe considers me precious and loved. I am truly blessed to be His daughter. I don't care what people think. God is my Father, my Friend, and my Judge.

2. Deuteronomy 32:10

_____

_____

_____

This Scripture shows me that I am _____.

Therefore I am special. The Holy God sees me as His precious possession.

3. Colossians 1:12

_____

_____

_____

This Scripture shows me that I am _____.

Therefore I am one of God's elect. What does the inheritance of the saints involve? Scripture says I will inherit the land (Ps. 37:29), I will inherit good things (Prov. 28:10), I will inherit all things (Rev. 21:7), I will inherit the kingdom prepared for me from the foundation of the world (Matt. 25:34), and I will inherit a blessing (1 Pet. 3:9). This inheritance is "incorruptible and undefiled" and "does not fade away." It is reserved for me in heaven (1 Pet. 4). No one is any richer or more blessed than I am.

4. Romans 8:37

_____

_____

_____

This Scripture shows me that I am _____.

Therefore I "can do all things through Christ who strengthens me" (Phil. 4:13). There is no reason for me to feel inferior.

Think about Esther. She was a Jewish orphan, a virtual nonentity. She had no particular promise. Yet the Book of Esther records, "Now the king was attracted to Esther more than to any of the other women, and she won his favor and approval more than any of the other virgins. So he set a royal crown on her head and made her queen instead of Vashti" (Esth. 2:17 NIV).

Why are you reluctant to accept the favor of God in your life, as Esther did? Mention the thoughts that might be holding you back below (like thinking that you don't deserve God's love):

_____

_____

_____

_____

What can you do to counteract those thoughts? Mention some ways below, like reminding yourself that you are one of God's elect (Col. 3:12):

_____

_____

_____

_____

Now look at the chart below to remind yourself of who you are as a daughter of the King.

WHO I AM AS A DAUGHTER OF THE KING

As a daughter of the King I have . . .

The mind of Christ: ". . . we have the mind of Christ" (1 Cor. 2:16).

Direct access to God. "Let us therefore come boldly to the throne of grace" (Heb. 4:16).

Power over Satan. "Behold, I give you the authority to trample . . . over all the power of the enemy, and nothing shall by any means hurt you" (Luke 10:19).

God's blessing. "All these blessings shall come upon you and overtake you" (Deut. 18:2).

We must watch our thoughts because they will become our words. We must watch our words because they will become our actions. We must watch our actions because they will mold our character. We must learn to see ourselves through the eyes of a loving God. When we see the potential He sees, then our character will mirror His.

In her book, *A Model for a Better Future*, Kim Alexis advises women to focus on inner beauty, not surface beauty. "On the outside, we are aging, we are losing our youth and our beauty day by day. But if we are focused on inner beauty, we can actually become more beautiful with each passing day. We can become more patient, more gentle, more compassionate, more strong, more truthful, more devoted, more gracious, more faithful, more Christlike with every new day.

"That's why, when I think of women I've known who are truly beautiful, I tend to think more of saintly, wise, wonderful women whose images would never be found on the cover of *Vogue*. They are women who may have little remaining of the youthful, outer beauty they had in their twenties—but they have acquired a depth of beauty that I truly want to have when I'm their age."[5]

I agree with Kim Alexis. Now I see my nose as an inheritance from my Heavenly Father. I wouldn't trade this feature for anything! Yes, ladies, as we reach our divine destiny, we will all become more beautiful!

Therefore, if anyone is in Christ, he is a new creation; old things have passed away; behold, all things have become new.

—2 CORINTHIANS 5:17

chapter three

I Am Not Ashamed of the Gospel:

The Power of My Testimony

"They overcame him by the blood of the Lamb and by the word of their testimony."

—Revelation 12:11

Each year some women come to the Woman of God sessions who haven't accepted Christ as Savior and given Him control of their lives. Some of these women have simply become too entangled with work and busyness to attend church or spend time with God in prayer. Others have wandered far away from Him. Nicole Stair was one of these women.

Nicole returned to San Antonio from Colorado where she had fallen into heavy drug use. She was pregnant and her mother had convinced her to come home so the family could support her and help her overcome her drug habit. Coincidently, a Woman of God class was held only a few weeks after she returned. Her grandmother, a faithful member of our church, suggested that Nicole attend the Woman of God class with her. I'm going to let Nicole tell you what happened in her own words.

"I was experiencing mood swings from the withdrawal from drugs. I used methamphetamine, cocaine, and other drugs. I didn't know what to do with myself so I said, 'Okay, I'll give it a try.'

"When we got into our discussion group, everyone was introducing themselves by saying, 'My name is _____.' And then telling why they were attending Woman of God. Reasons like 'I'm here because I think this is a really good chance to know myself and God.'

"I was really nervous. I thought, *Oh, here it goes. When I say I'm a drug addict everyone is just going to stare at me with an unspoken question in their eyes, 'What are you doing here?'* Still I told the women 'My name is Nicole Stair, and I'm a drug addict. I'm here because I want to try to change my life by knowing God, and I think maybe He can bless me by getting me over my drug addiction.'

"When I said that, the five women started clapping. I thought that was really strange. I'd never had that kind of support and love before."

That's the type of environment we mean to create in the Woman of God class. A supportive, nonjudgmental opportunity for seekers to respond to God's love and accept Christ as Savior.

During the sessions Nicole attended I asked the women, "Do you know that you are saved and that your name is written in the Lamb's Book of Life?"

I can ask a woman this question, "Are you saved?" and nine times out of ten she will answer yes. Yet when I ask the same person, "Have you prayed the Sinner's Prayer? Are you absolutely certain that your name is written in the Lamb's Book of Life?" the answer is rarely in the affirmative.

Why is that? It's simply that this woman has never received Jesus Christ into her heart. Salvation is not a denominational doctrine or a family inheritance. Salvation is a personal experience.

I gave Nicole and the other women in the Woman of God class the opportunity to go through the steps of salvation if they had any doubt about their salvation, and I give you, the reader, the same opportunity. (And if you are saved, you will want to walk through the process so you can remember the way to bring another person to Christ.)

Four steps are necessary to accept Christ as Savior. Work through these steps and the Scriptures that inspired them:

Step One: Admit that you are a sinner. Look up Isaiah 53:6 in the Bible and write this verse in the space below:

_____

_____

_____

_____

As you think about this Scripture, look at your life. Have you sinned, as Scripture says? To begin with, test yourself against the Ten Commandments in Exodus 20:1–17, which aren't ten suggestions as our culture seems to have dubbed them. Check the ones where you may have strayed:

_____ "I have no other gods but God Himself." (For instance, you do not worship possessions or addictions, like alcohol or drugs. You have total trust in God.)

_____ "I only worship the Lord, my God." (I bow down to no one or nothing else. I do not worship my husband and expect him to be my god.)

_____ "I only use God's name in ways that honor Him. I do not swear."

_____ "I rest on Sunday and do not work on that day. Instead I think about the Lord and His ways."

_____ "I respect and honor my parents."

_____ "I do not take another person's life. I protect and respect human life."

_____ "I have not committed adultery. I am true to my husband."

_____ "I have not stolen. I do not take what belongs to other people."

_____ "I have not lied about other people or gossiped about them."

_____ "I do not covet other people's possessions or their abilities at work. I am satisfied with what I have."

Now think about the areas that you have checked and list your specific sins on page 00. The beauty of being a King's daughter is that you need no intermediary. You can go directly to the throne of God.

A PRIVATE TALK WITH GOD

Lord, these are the unconfessed sins of my past . . .

_____

_____

_____

_____

_____

_____

_____

Lord, these are the sins I am presently committing . . .

_____

_____

_____

_____

_____

_____

_____

Are you sorry for these sins?

Repentance is a necessary part of this first step. Repentance means to turn your back, walk away, and decide not to do this again. If you are ready to do so, write a prayer of repentance in the space below.

*Lord Jesus, I know that You died on the Cross so that
my sins would be forgiven. I am sorry for . . .*

_____

_____

_____

_____

Now tear this page out of your workbook. God no longer remembers them and neither should you. They no longer exist!

Your Heavenly Father has forgiven your sins. Hear Him saying to you, "I will forgive your iniquity and your sin I will remember no more" (Jer. 31:34). God has forgotten your sins—and so should you. They no longer exist!

Step Two: Admit that you can do nothing to save yourself from sinning. Look up Isaiah 64:6 in the Bible and write the passage in the space below:

_____

_____

_____

_____

Is this true in your life? Did you score perfectly on that Ten Commandments test?

If you are like me, the answer is no. I try, but I slip. And I am not alone. The apostle Paul also struggled with this. He said, "I do not understand what I do. For what I want to do I do not do, but what I hate I do. . . . So I find this law at work: When I want to do good, evil is right there with me. For in my inner being I delight in God's law; but I see another law at work in the members of my body, waging war against the law of my mind and making me a prisoner of the law of sin at work within my members" (Rom. 7:15; 21–23, NIV).

If you are like Paul and me and are unable to save yourself from sinning, confess this in a prayer below:

Dear Father, I can't do this alone. I need You. Help me to . . .

_____

_____

_____

_____

Step Three: Realize that Jesus Christ was born, crucified, and resurrected to save lost people from their sins. Write Romans 5:8 in the space below:

_____

_____

_____

Now think about how your sin affects God and His Son, Jesus Christ. Scripture gives us some clues. After the prophet Isaiah describes our sinful state—"All we like sheep have gone astray"—God shows him Jesus' sacrifice:

> He was oppressed and He was afflicted,
> Yet He opened not His mouth;
> He was led as a lamb to the slaughter,
> And as a sheep before its shearers is silent,
> So He opened not his mouth. . . .
> He was cut off from the land of the living;
> For the transgressions of My people He was stricken.
> And they made His grace with the wicked (Is. 53:7–9).

Are you willing to accept Jesus' sacrifice for your sins? If so, write a prayer thanking Him for what He has done for you. God is responsible for every good moment in your life. Begin thanking Him for such simple blessings as the breath in your lungs in the space below:

> *Precious Lord, I thank You for the simple blessings of this*
> *beautiful day. I thank You for . . .*

_____

_____

_____

_____

_____

Step Four: Believe God's Word and invite Christ into your heart by faith. Write Jesus' words to His disciples in John 5:24 in the space below:

_____

_____

_____

Do you believe what Jesus says here? If so, seal your salvation by praying the following prayer of salvation:

Lord, I ask that You forgive me of all my sins, both known and unknown. I ask that You accept me as Your own and write my name in the Lamb's Book of Life. From this day forward I will read Your Word and obey it. Because of the blood of the Cross, I am now forgiven. My sins are buried in the sea of forgetfulness, never to be remembered against me anymore. I am now a child of God, the daughter of the King, and Jesus Christ is the Lord of my life. Amen.

Now your name is written in the Lamb's Book of Life. No one can blot it out. You are His. You will spend eternity with the Father in heaven. And so will Nicole Stair since she also prayed that prayer at the Woman of God class.

The heavenly hosts are celebrating this moment in your life right now. And so is the Lord Jesus Christ.

And what is your reward for accepting Christ as Savior? Scripture says:
Eye has not seen, nor ear heard,
Nor have entered into the heart of man

The things which God has prepared for those who love Him" (1 Cor. 2:9).

Once you have been redeemed you have the obligation to redeem others with your testimony, a testimony you are not afraid to give about a God of whom you are not ashamed. Before Jesus left this earth, He commanded His disciples: "Go therefore and make disciples of all the nations, baptizing them in the name of the Father and of the Son and of the Holy Spirit, teaching them to observe all things that I have commanded you; and lo, I am with you always, even to the end of the age" (Matt. 28:19–20).

Jesus meant this commandment for all those who follow Him, then and now. Yet many of us have a difficult time witnessing to others about the saving power of our God.

Think about your own life and check the statements below that apply to you:

_____ "I do not feel that Jesus is worth sharing with others."

_____ "I go to church on Sunday and I live a Christian life. I don't need to witness."

_____ "Religion and politics are two subjects that we are supposed to avoid. We live in a country where there is the separation of church and state."

_____ "I am afraid of looking foolish and being rejected by those I witness to."

I tend to be a people pleaser. I want people to like me, and I want people to want to be around me. So I was hesitant to share the gospel with others. Yet the Lord finally gave me this choice: Will you be a people pleaser or a Father pleaser?

I chose to be a Father pleaser, and I've never been sorry about that decision.

Leighton Ford, an internationally known evangelist and the president of Leighton Ford Ministries, which specializes in developing young Christian leaders worldwide, has written a book about the way to reach people for Christ, *The*

Power of Story. Ford says, "Each of us has a story—what I call 'a story with a small *s*,' the story of our own lives. At some point in our journey through life, our story collides with the Story of God—'the Story with a large *S*.' God's Story calls our story into question. We must make a choice: either to reject the Story of God or to merge our story with His Story."[1]

That's our salvation experience. And when we receive Christ, we become a *storyteller*, Ford says. "The Story produces a Vision, which then transforms Character, resulting in evangelism. This process—Story—Vision—Character—Evangelism—provides us with a clear, workable biblical pattern for effective, natural witnessing."[2]

Ford goes on to explain, "When the Story of God has produced a vision within us of who God is and what He wants to do in our lives, our character will be transformed in such a way that our witness—the telling of our stories—will be a natural outgrowth of who we are, a result of the transformed character God has produced in us. We will not be able to keep from telling our stories, because we are our stories. When people encounter us, they will see the Story written upon our lives."[3]

> The three dimensions of the Story of God are:
> The love of the Father
> The grace of the Son
> The fellowship of the Holy Spirit.[4]

We will talk about two of them in this chapter. The third will be discussed in Chapter Four, "The Holy Spirit and Me."

1. The Love of the Father

Ford says that people today are longing to hear our Story, a Story that says, "God made you, and you matter to God."[5] Many people today have never felt unconditional love, particularly the love of their fathers. God's love, the love of the Father, will reach them, he says.

How do we show others the love of God? Through our actions, Leighton Ford says. It's as simple as that.

"When people around us see our transformed character, when they see the way we love others with the Father's unique brand of unconditional *agape* love, when they see the trusting way we pray and live out our lives, then they will see God's Story written in our lives. Evangelism in a postmodern age must take on the character not only of *speaking* the truth, but of *modeling* the truth on a daily basis. People will know what kind of Father we have as they see what kind of sons and daughters *we* are, what kind of fathers and mothers *we* are, what kind of husbands and wives *we* are, what kind of supervisors and employers *we* are, what kind of teachers and mentors *we* are. . . . They must see the vibrant, dynamic character of God's people. They must see real integrity and consistency in Christians. They must see faithful covenant love in fathers and families and churches.

"When our love is like God's own unconditional agape love, people can't help but be challenged, because the Father's love is completely unlike the love of this world.

"When our generation comes face-to-face with the character of God's people, the story of their lives will collide head-on with the Story of God. Their own stories will be called into question. They will be forced to reexamine their lives, their values and the foundations of their beliefs. And many will be convinced, and will make a decision to merge their stories with the Greatest Story Ever Told."[6]

Nicole Stair felt God's love in our Woman of God sessions. Again I will let her tell you how this happened:

"During our first session we exchanged phone numbers and wrote them in our class book. We made a pact with each other. If any of us needed help, we would call someone in the class.

"About a week later I was going through a really hard time, and I decided to call Melissa, because she had seemed really, really nice. I was pregnant and I told her that I was really depressed. I didn't have anything for the baby.

"'Sometimes I feel like going back to drugs,' I admitted. 'Maybe it would be better if I just gave up my baby.' Melissa didn't hang up on me. Instead she began assuring me that God would be with me.

"During the twelve weeks of our classes, my discussion group gave me a baby shower to help me get clothes and supplies for my baby. They made me feel like I did not have to have drugs in my life to have fun or even have a smile on my face."

What about your life? How have your character and your actions expressed God's Story to others? List those ways below:

Father, I try to show Your love every day in these ways . . .

_____

_____

_____

_____

Are there some ways that you fail to express God's character in the way you relate to your husband, your children, people at work or in the community? List those ways below:

Lord, forgive me for the ways I have failed to show Your love, such as . . .

_____

_____

_____

_____

Write a prayer, asking God to help you overcome these tendencies in the space below:

Father God of hope and new beginnings, help me to show Your love by . . .

_____

_____

_____

_____

2. The Grace of the Son

The Story of God is also a story of grace. The Bible is not filled with saintly people. Instead we find people who have committed sins: adultery (King David) and lying (Abraham), for instance. Yet God loved them and gave them a second chance. Scripture tells us that David was a man after God's own heart. And God so loved us that He gave His only Son that we might be saved (John 3:16).

Leighton Ford says, "The Story of God's grace must not only be told in words. We must communicate not only with a clear voice, but with the authentic touch of grace. Our evangelism must be a hands-on evangelism, in which we roll up our sleeves and dare to touch human lives."[7]

How about you? Are there ways you can show God's grace to non-Christians? List those ways below:

_____

_____

_____

_____

Could God be calling you to reach out to a particular neighbor or friend? Remember before you can give your testimony, you must be a testimony.

Think about those around you and list three people who would benefit from God's grace and how you might reach them:

_____

_____

_____

Leighton Ford reminds his readers that evangelism is accomplished by "gracious conversation," a two-way conversation. "I have asked many Christians how they were brought to Christ, what kind of person witnessed to them, and what kind of conversation they had. Again and again it has been confirmed to me that the person who witnesses most effectively tends to listen about 80 percent of the time and talk only about 20 percent of the time."[8]

Ford uses Jesus' conversations with the Samaritan woman as an example. She speaks four times as many words as Jesus does. Unfortunately many Christians see evangelism as talking rather than listening.

And Ford also suggests that Christians should ask permission to tell their story. "When I ask Christians how they were brought to Christ, one comment I frequently hear is: 'The person who witnessed to me asked my permission to share the gospel. It was not an unrequested monologue. I didn't feel threatened or defensive by being buttonholed with the gospel. I felt valued and affirmed because this person was considerate of my time and my feelings.'"[9]

And obviously to tell our story we must be able to tell the difference Christ has made in our lives, our testimony. To do so, we need to compare our life before Christ to our life after His salvation.

I tell the women in the Woman of God sessions to ask the Lord to give them wisdom and guidance as they write their testimonies. The Lord promises, "If any of you lacks wisdom, let him ask of God, who gives to all liberally and without reproach, and it will be given to him" (James 1:5).

Take a moment now to write a prayer in the space below:

Dear Lord, direct my thoughts as I begin to think about the difference
You have made in my life. Help me to . . .

_____

_____

_____

_____

Then I tell the women to follow a three-point outline:

• My life before I received Christ.
• How I received Christ.
• My life after I received Christ.

Nicole Stair has a strong testimony as to how her life changed after she received Christ. She went into labor during one of the last Woman of God classes. A few days after the baby was born, she saw a guy throw a roach (street language for a joint) on the floor right outside her apartment. Nicole said, "The Jones of my drug cells came out and told me to pick up the joint. I put it to my lips and sucked in. That's when I knew I was doing something wrong. I just knew it.

"I was never that disgusted with myself until that day. I threw the joint down and stepped on it and stepped on it until it was mush. There was nothing left. Then I ran inside and told my mom, 'You wouldn't believe what I just did.'

"She asked, 'What did you do?'

"'The devil got a hold of me, and he gave me my Jones druggy cells back. He told me, 'Pick that joint up. Smoke it!' But I took one puff and that was it. I didn't even need to talk to the Lord. Can you believe that?'

"My mom said, 'You know what? God did help you, and He was there. That's what made you drop the joint.'

"I knew then that being at Cornerstone and going to Woman of God and being a part of a cell group was working for me. I knew my prayers were being heard and that my daily Bible reading was making a difference to me."

This story of Nicole's redemption and your story are the verbal part of reaching people for Christ. You have probably witnessed to God's Story—His unconditional love and grace—to this person before the moment when you tell *your* story, which gives your testimony greater validity.

Often people will reciprocate. They will tell you their story—their pain, their struggles, and the hopelessness they feel—after they've heard *your* story. I often end my testimony with the question: "Has this ever happened to you?"

This is when we need to listen, truly listen, to their story. Then they will be open to the gospel as we present it through the Scriptures.

Take your Bible and mark the passages in the four steps to salvation.

THE FOUR STEPS OF SALVATION

Step One: Admit that you are a sinner (Is. 53:6).

Step Two: Admit that you can do nothing to save yourself from sinning (Is. 64:6).

Step Three: Realize that Jesus Christ was born, crucified, and resurrected to save lost people from their sins (Rom. 5:8).

Step Four: Believe God's Word and invite Christ into your heart by faith (John 5:24).

Write the first verse at the front of your Bible. Then note the next verse beside each of the passages. Now your Bible is a map you can use to guide someone through the plan of salvation.

It is important for all of us to give our testimony with the purpose of bringing others to the saving knowledge of Jesus Christ. However, it is not our responsibility if the person hears our testimony and then refuses to receive the Lord Jesus as Savior. This person has chosen to reject Christ. God has given human beings that right. Since the Garden of Eden, women have been making choices for their good or for their detriment. Not all will choose Christ, but you may be surprised by how many will do so.

In his book, *The Power of Story*, Leighton Ford suggests that people read through the Book of Acts in one sitting so they can see what God can do and what He wants to do through each of us. Ford says, "You'll see that this is not the story of evangelists and church leaders sitting down to develop grand strategies. No human being or committee of human beings could have planned the amazing course of events that we see in this book. Rather, what we see is the Story of the sovereign Spirit closing this door and opening that door, while the early Christians say, 'Look what God the Evangelist is doing! How are we going to be part of this?'"[10]

Our God is a good God. He wants us to prosper in all things. I call Him the God of two choices. He sets before us life and death and tells us to choose life. He sets before us blessings and curses and tells us to choose blessings. He wants the best for us. We receive His best when we are obedient. I ask you to obey His desire to make you a fisher of lost souls. Once you do, your life will take on a worth that is far greater than rubies. You will be a valued partner with Christ as together you bring the lost to the throne of a loving God. Choose to be a Father pleaser.

Turn to page 212 in Part Two and work through these steps to prepare your personal testimony, which is in Lesson Three.

"You are the light of the world. A city that is set on a hill cannot be hidden.

"Nor do they light a lamp and put it under a basket, but on a lampstand, and it gives light to all who are in the house.

"Let your light so shine before men, that they may see your good works and glorify your Father in heaven."

—MATTHEW 5:14–16

chapter four

The Holy Spirit and Me:

Walking in Divine Power

"What is the exceeding greatness of His power toward us who believe."
—Ephesians 1:19

*I*n my book *The King's Daughter* I said that every one of us needs to ask a question in the privacy of our prayer closet: Do I have all of God I want? I admitted that I am a very practical person. I want to know what God wants me to know. I want to have what He wants me to have. I want to do what He wants me to do. If there is more of Him, then I want it.

In the chapter on the Holy Spirit I talked about four different benefits of the baptism of the Holy Spirit: the power to be an effective witness, the power to pray according to God's will, the power to understand God's Word, and the power to experience the pouring out of God's love.

Now I would like to add three more benefits to that list. The Holy Spirit gives us the power to know God's will and obey Him, to live a consistent life, and to discern truth from error.

1. The Power to Know God's Will and Obey

Scripture makes it very clear that we cannot know God's will without the power of the Holy Spirit. The apostle Paul could see how the Holy Spirit helps us to know God's thoughts.

The Ability to Know God's Thoughts

Paul explained to the Corinthian church that when he had visited them he had only taught them the simple truth of Christ's life and His death. But in this epistle he would tell them about "the secret wisdom of God" (1 Cor. 2, 7 NLT). He said:

> But we know these things because God has revealed them to us by his Spirit, and his Spirit searches out everything and shows us even God's deep secrets. No one can know what anyone else is really thinking except that person alone, and no one can know God's thoughts except God's own Spirit. And God has actually given us his Spirit (not the world's spirit) so we can know the wonderful things God has freely given us. When we tell you this, we do not use words of human wisdom. We speak words given to us by the Spirit, using the Spirit's words to explain spiritual truths. But people who aren't Christians can't understand these truths from God's Spirit. It all sounds foolish to them because only those who have the Spirit can understand what the Spirit means. We who have the Spirit understand these things, but others can't understand us at all. How could they? For 'Who can know what the Lord is thinking? Who can give him counsel?' But we can understand these things, for we have the mind of Christ" (1 Cor. 2:10–16, NLT).

Note the prerequisite here: "only those who have the Holy Spirit can understand what the Holy Spirit means." If we want to know God's Will, we must have the Holy Spirit. Only then do we have the mind of Christ. Only then will the Holy Spirit show us God's deep secrets.

Jesus also made it clear that the Holy Spirit was necessary for us to know God's will. He told the disciples, "I am telling you these things now while I am still with you. But when the Father sends the Counselor as my representative—and by the Counselor I mean the Holy Spirit—he will teach you everything and will remind you of everything I myself have told you" (John 14:26 NLT).

And Jesus repeated this fact again when he said, "I still have many things to say to you, but you cannot bear them now. However, when He, the Spirit of truth, has come, He will guide you into all truth; for He will not speak on His own authority, but whatever He hears He will speak; and He will tell you things to come. He will glorify Me, for He will take of what is Mine and declare it to you" (John 16:12–14).

If we want all of God's truth, we need the power of the Holy Spirit.

Are you being sensitive to God's will in your life? If so, note a time when you sensed God's will for you in the space below:

_____

_____

_____

_____

What led you to believe this was God's will for you? Note that in the space below:

_____

_____

_____

_____

Are you willing to obey God's will for your life and to obey God's Word? That's a very important question because obedience determines your spiritual destiny. The rich young ruler asked Jesus, "What shall I do to inherit eternal life?"

Jesus asked the young ruler if he had obeyed the Ten Commandments and he said, "All these I have kept from my youth" (Luke 18:21).

Jesus made one final stipulation: "Sell all you have and give it to the poor." This rich young ruler had kept the Ten Commandments, but he could not obey Jesus.

Throughout His ministry Jesus identified His disciples as those who heard His words and did them. Many people hear God's Word, they even believe it's true, but they do not have the power to obey. Yet we lose our credentials as Christians if we don't obey.

Let me ask you again. Are you willing to obey God's will for your life and to obey His Word? _____ yes _____ no. If so, write a prayer in the space below, asking God to help you to do so:

Dear Lord, I ask You to help me to obey Your will for my life through the power of Your Holy Spirit. . . .

_____

_____

_____

The Holy Spirit also gives us the power to live a consistent Christian life.

2. The Power to Live a Consistent Christian Life

The first way the Holy Spirit gives us this power is by guiding us away from the wrong places and to the right ones.

The Holy Spirit Can Guide Us.

Scripture tells us that after Paul and Silas traveled through the area of Phrygia and Galatia, the Holy Spirit told them not to preach the Word in Asia. Paul must have thought that since he couldn't go south into the province of Asia, he would go north. So he headed to Mysia. Paul and Silas set out for the province of Bithynia. "But again the spirit of Jesus did not let them go" (Acts 16:6 NLT). The Holy Spirit had told Paul not to go south, now he was told not to go north. And he had come from the east, so there was only one direction to go—west. And that's what he did: "So instead, they went on through Mysia to the city of Troas" (Acts 16:7). Paul had to stop there since he was right on the Aegean Sea. I'm sure Paul probably wondered what he should do next.

In his book, *Thru the Bible*, J. Vernon McGee describes Paul's dilemma this way: "I think that if we had met Paul during the time of his delay in Troas, we could have asked him, 'Paul, where are you going?' I'm sure his reply would have been, 'I don't know.' I'm afraid our next statement would have been something like this: 'Now brother Paul, do you mean that the great Apostle of the Gentiles doesn't know where he is going next? Surely you must know the will of God for your life.' Then we would have sat down for a nice long lecture on how to determine the will of God in his life. My, I've read so many books on that subject—it's too bad Paul didn't have one of those books with him at that time! Paul does not know the will of God. Why? Because the *Spirit of God* is leading him. Paul is simply waiting. It is going to take a mighty movement to get Paul out of Asia and move him over into Europe."[1] Remember this: When you don't know what to do *wait.*

And the Holy Spirit did guide Paul. Scripture tells us what happened next: "That night Paul had a vision. He saw a man from Macedonia in northern Greece, pleading with him, 'Come over here and help us' so we decided to leave for Macedonia at once, for we could only conclude that God was calling us to preach the Good News there" (Acts 16:8–10 NLT).

J. Vernon McGee says he is thankful that the Holy Spirit sent Paul to Europe. "I do not know why Paul was not moved east to China. All I know is that the Spirit of God moved him west to Europe. I thank God that this is the direction he went. At that particular time, my ancestors from one side of the family, were roaming in the forests of Germany. They were pagan and they were evil, worshiping all kinds of idols. They were a low, heathen people. . . . At any rate, I am told they were the dirtiest, filthiest savages that have ever been on the topside of this earth. I thank God the gospel went to Europe to reach my people over there.

"Now maybe you are smiling, thinking that your ancestors were very superior to mine. Well, you can wipe that smile off your face because your ancestors probably were living in the cave right next door to mine! They were just as dirty and just as filthy as mine were. Thank God the gospel crossed over into Europe. This was a great and significant crossing."[2]

Paul was attuned to the Holy Spirit's guidance as he traveled throughout the first-century world. And what a difference this made to all of us.

We should also be watching for the Holy Spirit's guidance in our lives today. Often the Holy Spirit will guide us to the right places, but He also guides us away from the wrong places.

Have you felt God guiding you away from wrong places? Note that experience in the space below:

_____

_____

_____

_____

If so, how did you know this was the Holy Spirit? Note that in the space below:

_____

_____

Have you ever felt God guiding you in the right direction? Note that in the space below:

_____

_____

_____

_____

Some people say that God closes one door and opens another one. Note a time in your life when that happened in the space below:

_____

_____

_____

_____

How did you know this was the Holy Spirit? Note how you knew this in the space below:

_____

_____

I've found that one way the Holy Spirit guides me is through a sense of peace or rightness about what I am doing and ill ease about what is not His will.

Jesus gave us another indication of the Holy Spirit's guidance. "However, when He, the Spirit of truth, has come, He will guide you into all truth; for He will not speak on His own authority, but whatever He hears He will speak; and He will tell you things to come. He will glorify Me, for He will take what is Mine and declare it to you" (John 16:13–14).

J. Vernon McGee points out two significant steps in this Scripture: the Holy Spirit will not speak of Himself and the Holy Spirit will glorify Jesus. McGee says that since we have these steps, we have a way of knowing if the Holy Spirit is at work.

Then McGee gives an example of how he himself did so. "I listened to a man on a radio program saying, 'We are having a Holy Ghost revival; the Holy Ghost is working; the Holy Ghost is doing this and that.' The minute he said all those things, I knew the Holy Ghost was not working. Why? Because the Lord Jesus made it very clear that the Holy Ghost will not speak of Himself. Then how can you tell when the Holy Spirit is working? He will glorify Christ. My friend, when in a meeting or a Bible study you suddenly get a glimpse of the Lord Jesus and He becomes wonderful, very real, and meaningful to you, that is the working of the Holy Spirit. Jesus said, 'He shall glorify *Me.*'"[3]

The Holy Spirit also helps us live a Christian life by guiding our words in difficult situations.

The Holy Spirit Can Teach Us What to Say

Jesus gave His disciples instructions before He sent them to preach to the Jews. He prepared them for the inevitable persecution by saying, "When you are arrested, don't worry about what to say in your defense, because you will be given the right words at the right time. For it won't be you doing the talking—it will be the Spirit of your Father speaking through you" (Matt. 10:19–20).

And this is exactly what happened when Peter had to speak about Christ before the Jewish council, men such as Annas, the high priest, after Peter healed the crippled man. Peter was so eloquent that "the members of the council were amazed when they saw the boldness of Peter and John, for they could see that they were ordinary men who had no special training" (Acts 4:8–14).

The Holy Spirit told Peter and John what to say, and the Holy Spirit also tells us today.

Many years ago when my husband was a young pastor, there was a long pause at the end of the Sunday morning service. He could feel the presence of the Holy Spirit in the sanctuary so he said, "God is trying to reach someone in this audience to receive Christ."

Again there was a long pause. John waited for a few more moments, then he felt the Holy Spirit telling him to say, "Someone in this audience has planned to take her life because of the desperate circumstances in which she finds herself. But if she would receive Christ today, every problem she thinks she is facing would be resolved and she would have eternal life."

As soon as my husband finished saying that, a middle-aged woman ran down the aisle. She opened her purse and pulled out a bottle of pills and a suicide note to her family.

Once the woman had stopped weeping, John led her in a prayer of confession of sin, and she received Christ as Savior. The Holy Spirit had given my husband the right words at the right time.

Think about your own life. Is there a time when the Holy Spirit gave you the right words at the right time? If so, note that experience in the space below:

_____

_____

_____

The Holy Spirit also gives us the power of discernment.

3. The Ability to Discern Truth from Error

The Holy Spirit helps us to discern false teaching, to know when someone is distorting God's truth. Christians throughout the ages have struggled to know what is true. In his first letter John warned the early Christians about the false teachers in the early church who were denying the Incarnation of Christ:

"I have written these things to you because you need to be aware of those who want to lead you astray. But you have received the Holy Spirit, and He lives within you, so you don't need anyone to teach you what is true. For the Spirit teaches you all things, and what He teaches is true—it is not a lie. So continue in what he has taught you, and continue to live in Christ" (1 John 2:26–27 NLT).

And John reiterated this again four chapters later when he said, "Beloved, do not believe every spirit, but test the spirits, whether they are of God; because many false prophets have gone out into the world" (1 John 4:1).

Was there a time when you needed discernment, a time when you questioned someone's interpretation of Scripture? If so, note that experience in the space below:

_____

_____

_____

_____

How did you discern the truth? Note that in the space below:

_____

_____

Often I feel uneasy in my spirit when someone is interpreting Scripture in an improper way. When I sense this, I run to Scripture to verify what is being said. Most Bibles have a section in the front or back called "Topical Index," which lists pertinent Scripture according to topic. For instance, when I was searching for the power of the Holy Spirit in my life, I looked in an index section under Holy Spirit.

If you feel you have encountered a false teacher, you might also want to understand the characteristics of such a person. In the Topical Index of the *New Open Bible Study Edition*, there is a listing "False teachers," which gives Scriptural references that show the characteristics of false teachers, the prevalence of false teachers, and examples of false teachers in the Bible.

My husband describes eleven characteristics of a wolf in sheep's clothing:

• Pride and egotism
• Arrogance
• Boastfulness
• Exaggeration
• Dishonesty
• Covetousness
• Financial irresponsibility
• Licentiousness
• Immorality
• Addictive appetites or habits
• Confusion in the home

The first thing a false teacher will tell you is, "Don't judge me." Yet you are not judging someone if you are checking his fruit. Jesus said, "Beware of false prophets, who come to you in sheep's clothing, but inwardly they are ravenous wolves. You will know them by their fruits" (Matt. 7:15–16). If you ascertain any of the above characteristics in a person whose message seems to vary from Scripture, listen to the Spirit of God within you and be wary of this person's teaching.

Remember, one of the most important decisions in your life will be to attend a strong Bible-believing church. A church whose pastor teaches and preaches out of the Word of God in an uncompromised way. A shepherd who ends his service with an altar call, inviting the lost to the throne of the living God to receive eternal life.

And what is the exceeding greatness of His power toward us who believe, according to the working of His mighty power . . .

—EPHESIANS 1:19

chapter five

Dreams with a Happy Ending:

Setting Goals

"Write the vision and make it plain."
—HABAKKUK 2:2

Someone has said, "Goals are dreams with a deadline." In my book *The King's Daughter* I gave seven steps to setting dreams that have a happy ending:

1. Have a vision for the future.
2. Make time to be with God.
3. Seek God's will for your life.
4. Write down your vision and make it plain.
5. Check your goals with the Word of God.
6. Stay focused on your vision: Don't give way to a defeated attitude.
7. Be willing to change if God desires it.

Now is the time to apply these steps to your goal-setting process.

THE GOAL-SETTING PROCESS

1. Have a Vision for the Future.

We learn from the Word of God that "Where there is no vision, the people perish" (Prov.29:18 KJV). Any goal-setting process is going to begin with a vision. *The American Heritage Dictionary* defines vision as "intelligent foresight."[1]

One of my parents' many visions for our family was to attain as many opportunities as this great country had to offer, and one of those blessings was a good education. My dad was an only child whose father died when he was nine. To help provide for himself and my grandmother, he had to drop out of school in the ninth grade and go to the migration fields in California to pick peaches. He knew how important an education would be for my sister and me, even though dad had overcome his educational deficiencies and finally supervised more than four hundred employees at Hughes Aircraft, most of whom were college graduates and some of whom held master's degrees in technology.

What is your vision for the future? Some say we should plan as if we had 1,000 years to live and live as if Jesus were coming today. What do you want to accomplish in the next year? Write that in the space below:

_____

_____

In the next five years:

_____

_____

Now it's time to ask God to confirm these ideas.

2. Make Time to Be with God.

Jesus' biological brother James wrote his epistle to teach early Christians how to live. He said:

> Look here, you people who say, "Today or tomorrow we are going to a certain town and will stay there a year. We will do business there and make a profit." How do you know what will happen tomorrow? For your life is like the morning fog—it's here a little while, then it's gone. What you ought to say is, "If the Lord wants us to, we will live and do this or that." Otherwise you will be boasting about your own plans, and all such boasting is evil (James 4:13–16 NLT).

Proverbs 3 also says, "Trust in the Lord with all your heart, and lean not on your own understanding. In all your ways acknowledge Him, and He shall direct your paths" (vv. 5–6).

Take a moment now to write a prayer, asking God to direct your goal-setting:

Dear Heavenly Father, Your Word says that You order our steps and that You will uphold us with Your hand, therefore I ask You to . . .

_____

_____

_____

Notice that I have suggested that you pray God's Word back to Him. Psalm 37:23–24 says, "The steps of a good man are ordered by the LORD, and He delights in his way. Though he fall, he shall not be utterly cast down; for the LORD upholds him with His hand." Often we can expect the Lord to honor our requests when we pray His Word back to Him.

In the next few days, take a moment during each of your prayer times to ask God to confirm your vision or redirect it in the path He has purposed for your life.

Do you feel as if God has confirmed your vision? If not, what do you think He is saying to you? Write that in the space below:

_____

_____

_____

Now ask yourself if this vision is a part of God's will for your life.

3. Seek God's Will for Your Life.

Let's begin this step by looking at God's ultimate goal for us. Paul told the early Roman Christians, "For God knew his people in advance, and he chose them to become like his Son, so that his Son would be the firstborn, with many brothers and sisters" (Rom. 8:29 NLT).

This goal is our ultimate objective as daughters of the King. We want to look like our brother Jesus.

Think about your own life. What can you do to look more like your brother Jesus? Set three spiritual goals that will help you to do this in the space below:

_____

_____

_____

Now you are ready for step four.

4. Write Down Your Vision and Make It Plain.

The book of Habbakuk instructs us about our vision:

I will stand my watch and set myself on the rampart, and watch to see what He will say to me, and what I will answer when I am corrected. Then the LORD answered me and said: "Write the vision down and make it plain on tablets, that he may run who reads it. For the vision is yet for an appointed time; but at the end it will speak, and it will not lie. Though it tarries, wait for it; because it will surely come, it will not tarry (Hab. 2:1–3).

You must understand what God is saying to you in this passage. Think through this Scripture with me:

What is God saying to you in verse one?

_____

_____

What is God saying to you in verse two?

_____

_____

What is God saying to you in verse three?

_____

_____

In Habbukuh 2 the Holy Spirit is telling us that He requires us to bring all of our problems, disappointments, and desires to Him, expecting His comfort, His answer, and His guidance in every situation. We must spend time listening to Him and His Word. Habbukuh says, "I will stand my watch and set myself on the rampart, and watch to see what He will say to me, and what I will answer when I am corrected" (v. 1).

Secondly, the Holy Spirit wants us to write our goals down and make them so clear that any man can understand them: "Write the vision down and make it plain on tablets" (v. 3). We need to go through the Word of God and record the promises He has proclaimed over our lives and trust that they are for us.

Thirdly, the Lord wants us to hold fast to our dreams, visions, and goals once they have been confirmed by His Word. He warns us not to get discouraged for the answers may "tarry," but they will be fulfilled: "For the vision is yet for an appointed time; but at the end it will speak, and it will not lie. Though it tarries, wait for it; because it will surely come, it will not tarry" (v. 3).

Have you been guilty of becoming discouraged and losing sight of your vision? I have. In this "quick-gratification" society it is easy to lose sight of our goals when they are not easily or quickly reached. In order to start anew with a fresh mind-set about the goals we want to set for our lives, let's begin with a prayer of repentance over our attitude.

> *Father, I ask that You forgive me for losing sight of my vision and becoming discouraged because I didn't think it came soon enough. I have opened the door to depression and defeat and I repent of not keeping my heart focused on You, Your Word, and Your promises. Today is a new day and I will covenant with You to hear Your voice and set my mind on the things You have ordained for my life. I will wait on Your provision as I do all that I can to reach my goals. In Jesus' Name. Amen.*

Now begin to write your goals. In *The King's Daughter* I gave a personal example of goal-setting. My paternal grandmother came to the United States when she was fifteen, but she never learned to speak English. Our family lived with my grandmother when I was born, and consequently I didn't learn English until I was almost six years old.

What a shock I received when our family moved to California where I entered the first grade. For the first time I encountered people who only spoke English. At the time when I should have been learning to read and write, I lost the ability to communicate. How could I get a good education, which was one of my parents' visions?

My mom and dad realized that this had to be changed. Our short-term goal became: Learn to speak English quickly.

Sometimes our goal should be to position ourselves wherever God is working, wherever His Holy Spirit is moving. Before recent elections I felt God was calling America to her knees to pray and seek His face. Therefore, I felt that one of my goals for that year was to spend time every day to pray for the elections.

When we set goals, we often need to pray "Lord, what is Your will for this moment in time? Let me be conformed and changed to submit myself to You and what You are doing."

Think about your short-term goals, ones that can be accomplished within the next year. Write those goals in the space below:

1. _____

2. _____

3. _____

Now begin to imagine how you will get from these goals to your vision. These are your long-term goals. Write three long-term goals that you want to accomplish in the next five years in the space below:

1. _____

2. _____

3. _____

5. Check Your Goals with the Word of God.

The Word of God is always at the core of any decision you may have for your life. Is what you are hearing in accordance with the Word of God or contrary to its teaching? Test your goals against these Scriptural injunctions.

Do All to the Glory of God.

We are commanded to do all to the glory of God: "Therefore, whether you eat or drink or whatever you do, do all to the glory of God" (1 Cor. 10:31). Look back at your three short-term goals. Do they glorify God? Place a checkmark beside the ones that do.

Now look back at your three long-term goals. Do they glorify God? Place a checkmark beside the ones that do. These are the goals you will keep.

Do Justly

Micah 6:8 says, "And what does the LORD require of you but to do justly?" Are your goals right for you and for those around you? Are your goals just? Again look back at the list of your goals on page 59. If any of your short-term or long-term goals are not right for you or those around you, put a line through them. Jesus said, "Whoever causes one of these little ones who believe in Me to sin, it would be better for him if a millstone were hung around his neck, and he were drowned in the depth of the sea" (Matt. 18:6–7).

Now that you have set good goals, you need to determine to see them through to completion.

6. Stay focused on your vision: Don't give way to a defeated attitude.
Let's begin with the step of staying focused on your vision.

Stay Focused

Don't give way to a defeated attitude. Remember what the book of Habakkuk says, "For the vision is yet for an appointed time; but at the end it will speak, and it will not lie. Though it tarries, wait for it; because it will surely come, it will not tarry" (Hab. 2:2–3).

When you are tempted to give way to a defeated attitude, read this verse again to remember that your vision might have an appointed time in the future. The Word of God instructs us to "wait for it."

To stay focused on your vision, you must list some action points to achieve that goal. My family's action point to achieve our goal of learning to speak English was to establish a rule in our home: No Spanish spoken here. And that goal had a reward: I learned to speak English properly and so excelled in school that I received an academic scholarship to one of the finest universities in the south, Trinity University.

With favor from God and much effort and dedication on my part, my parents' vision was achieved: I became the first person on my father's side of the family and the first woman on my mother's side of the family to receive a college education. If my parents hadn't set that goal or implemented the action point, I'm not sure how I would have succeeded.

Write your action points to reach each goal. For example, is one of your goals to get out of debt? Then you should prepare a budget as your action point. You should pray and ask God to give you wisdom as to how you can creatively and realistically reach your desired goal.

Write your three short-term goals in the space below and then the action points you need to achieve those goals.

1. Short-Term Goal:_____

_____

_____

2. Short-Term Goal:_____

_____

_____

3. Short Term Goal:_____

_____

_____

Now write your three long-term goals in the space below and then the action points you need to achieve those goals, knowing you will need God's direction, wisdom, and favor to accomplish them.

1. Long-Term Goal:_____

_____

_____

2. Long-Term Goal: _____

_____

_____

3. Long-Term Goal: _____

_____

_____

We have begun down the path of goal-setting. You should go through this same process for all the goals you set so you make them a part of the rest of your life. Remember, "without a vision the people perish."

Now let's consider how you will remain focused on your goals when obstacles occur and you are tempted to give in to a defeated attitude.

REMAIN FOCUSED DESPITE OBSTACLES

As a pastor's wife I sit on the pew to support my husband, but I also sit there to be blessed by his sermons. One of his most life changing sermons for me was about God's promises. In every believer's life we find a promise that applies to our situation in the Word of God. Inevitably a problem (an obstacle) will be linked to that promise.

My husband began this sermon with the example of the Hebrew slaves who were promised they would be led out of Egypt to a land flowing with milk and honey (their vision). My husband said, "The greater the promise, the greater the problem! If God gives you a million dollar promise, you will have a million dollar problem!"

However, John told our members, "How you react to the problem determines how long the problem will remain in your life. The children of Israel became rebellious; they murmured and complained. I can hear them saying, 'We remember the fish we used to eat in Egypt. We remember the leeks and garlic, the tacos and jalapeno peppers. The grits and fat back. Now all we have to eat is this manna!' The Israelites were a stiff-necked people like some church members.

"Therefore their problem remained with them for forty years, until those stiff-necked people were dead. When you disobey God in the problem, He doesn't sit in heaven, wringing His hands and drinking Maalox®. He doesn't say, 'Oh, my. What shall I do? They're not obeying me.' Instead His response is, 'Take another lap around Mt. Sinai.'

"The purpose of the problem is not to discourage you, as you think. God's purpose is to develop you. Problems are living proof that you are a card-carrying member of the human race.

"Do you have a problem?" John asked. "Fantastic! Shout hallelujah. You're in a perfect position to discover the power of God to:

- Make a way where there seems to be no way.
- Make the crooked path straight.
- Remove the mountains and lift up the valleys.
- Receive houses you didn't build, wells you didn't dig, vineyards you didn't plant.

"You may run from problems, you may complain about problems, but problems have made you what you are. Teach yourself a therapeutic phrase: Get over it! Think about the mighty oak tree. A tiny seed has to struggle and push its way through the rock and hard soil to find sunshine and air. Then this small seedling has to wrestle with storms and snow and frost *before* it becomes a mighty oak. The purpose of the problem is to motivate you to a new level of accomplishment!"

I remember my husband's words each time I encounter a problem. Think about your own life. What difficulties might you encounter on your way to achieving your goals? Think about those obstacles now so you can plan for them in the future.

Begin with one of your short-term goals for the next year. List the short-term goal and then the obstacles you may be facing in the space below:

Short-Term Goal: _____

_____

_____

_____

Now think about how you can overcome these problems. List some ways in the space below:

_____

_____

Then go on to one of your long-term goals. What could keep you from achieving this goal? List the long-term goal and then the obstacles in the space below:

Long-Term Goal: _____

_____

_____

_____

Now think about how you can overcome these problems. List some ways in the space below:

_____

_____

_____

You are prepared for the days ahead. Begin now to work toward those goals, but be willing to change if God desires it.

7. Be Willing to Change If God Desires It.

Proverbs 16:9 says, "A man's heart plans his way, but the LORD directs his steps."

Sometimes our plans may not lead us to the Lord's ultimate destination.

Most of us think that a man like John Ashcroft, the former Attorney General of the United States, completed all his goals quickly and shot right to the top. Not so. John Ashcroft was always willing to make a detour if he thought God desired it.

Ashcroft began as a college professor. In 1972, when there was only one announced Republican candidate in his congressional district, he decided to run for a seat in Congress. He only garnered about 45 percent of the vote in the primary campaign so he lost the nomination. He went back to teaching college students, but God had other plans.

In the next month, Kit Bond who was the governor-elect of Missouri called Ashcroft. He told Ashcroft that he should think about state government and asked John to send a resume to him. At the time John didn't remember that Kit had been the state auditor when he ran for governor, and he would soon need to appoint someone to fill his old office. John Ashcroft was his choice. He was being handed the fourth-ranking job in the state without even asking for it! This is what I would call a divine appointment.

Ashcroft sees a series of "crucifixions and resurrections" throughout his life. If losing the election for Congress was a crucifixion, then his appointment as state auditor was a resurrection. There is only one state auditor in Missouri, but there are nine congressional representatives. This opened the door to a lifelong vocation of public service. But this vocation also held other detours.

In 1974 Ashcroft ran for a second term as state auditor. Again he lost an election. Even though he had held the fourth-highest state office at thirty, he still had to win an election by the age of thirty-three.

Two years later he decided to try again, even though he had lost two previous elections. This time he ran for state attorney general. And this time he won, even though Kit Bond narrowly lost his bid for reelection and Jimmy Carter defeated incumbent president, Gerald Ford.

In the 90s, his failure to be elected chairman of the Republican National Committee led to his successful race for United States Senate. And in 2000 when he lost the Republican nomination for president of the United States, George W. Bush asked him to serve as attorney general.

Ashcroft acknowledges, "We don't like the losses in life. They don't leave behind the sweet aftertaste of victory. Sometimes they leave us feeling nothing more than the sore muscles of defeat. But those sore muscles signify that growth is taking place, leading to something even better. . . . As we travel through the peaks of acclaim and the valleys of rejection, and as we watch our children do the same, we can take heart that it is the journey, not just the destination, that carries meaning and fulfillment."[2]

How about you? Are you willing to make a detour if God desires it? If so, write a prayer in the space below, giving the Lord full authority over your vision and your goals:

Dear Lord, Your Word says that You know the plans
You have for me. Therefore I give You . . .

And know that wherever God leads you, in whatever position He places you, you can serve on Holy Ground.

The night before John Ashcroft was sworn into the Senate in 1995, his father arranged for some close friends and family members to gather for dinner. John's dad asked that John play the hymn "We Are Standing on Holy Ground."

Just as Moses could stand in the barren wilderness of the Sinai Peninsula and hear God proclaim it holy ground, John's father wanted him to stand in the citadel of human power and say, "This place should be set apart for the work of the Lord."

After the song was finished, Robert Ashcroft said, "John, I want you to know that even Washington can be holy ground. It's a place to hear the voice of God, and wherever you hear His voice, that ground is sanctified, or set apart. It's a place where God can call you to the highest and best."[3]

In his book *On My Honor*, John Ashcroft says, "In my father's view—and I think he was right in this—the factory floor in Detroit can be holy ground; the stock market exchange on Wall Street can be holy ground; the local elementary school; the first hall; the Elks lodge; even the chew-'em-up-and-spit-'em-out halls of Washington, D.C.

"The more I invite God's presence into whatever I do, the more likely I will reflect His Spirit, and nothing is more meaningful than that."[4]

Let me end this chapter on goal-setting with these words that can guide us as we plan our journey in the years ahead:

Learn from your yesterdays.

Live for today.

Hope for your tomorrow.

I do not count myself to have apprehended; but one thing I do, forgetting those things which are behind and reaching forward to those things which are ahead, I press toward the goal for the prize of the upward call of God in Christ Jesus.

—PHILIPPIANS 3:13–14

chapter six

Women in the Workplace:

Be Diligent in All Things

"Let each one examine his own work."

—GALATIANS 6:4

*I*n my book *The King's Daughter*, I gave the Ten Commandments of Women in the Workplace. In this chapter I'd like to consider additional Scriptures that guide our conduct, whether we work at home or outside the home. I believe all women are members of the workforce; every woman is a working woman. No matter what the circumstances, her work is never done.

The American Heritage Dictionary defines *work* as "physical or mental effort or activity directed toward the production or accomplishment of something." This basic definition of work clearly indicates that it requires effort and action on our part. We work because we were created to work: "Six days shall you labor and do all your work" (Ex. 20:9)[1]

The writer of Psalms set the parameters of work when he said, "Man goes out to his work and to his labor until evening" (Ps. 104:23).

Scripture describes a Christian's attitude toward work: We are to work heartily and to persevere in our work. Then we can expect to be rewarded.

1. Work Heartily

Paul told the Colossian Christians: "And whatever you do, do it heartily, as to the Lord and not to men, knowing that from the Lord you will receive the reward of the inheritance; for you serve the Lord Christ" (Col. 3:23–24).

That implies real dedication (but not an overzealous obsession with work). You will remember Judy, the single mom who was so overwhelmed by raising three children by herself. Judy had been a stay-at-home mom for sixteen years; she felt she had little ability to enter the marketplace. But the Lord had a different plan in mind. As you read Judy's account of her entrance into the workforce notice her determination to improve herself and her willingness to work "heartily."

JUDY'S WORK EXPERIENCE

Judy told me how she got a job after sixteen years of being a stay-at-home mom. "One day I went to my best friend Kelly's home after I dropped both of our kids off at church to attend a youth retreat, and her husband, Scott, was there."

Kelly and Scott were sitting together at the table and Judy admitted that she needed a job. Scott asked her, "Well, what can you do?"

"I used to be a secretary," Judy said. Then she admitted, "But I don't know how to work a computer. I've been trying to teach myself, but I'm not proficient at it, by any means."

"Well, can you answer the phone?"

"Yes, I could do that," Judy answered.

"Well, let me talk to my partner, Brian. I'll call you on Monday."

Two days later Scott asked Judy to come for an interview. The small company worked on turbine engines for small planes. Their office only had eleven employees and a phone with four lines. They were willing to hire Judy to answer the phone. She had very few skills when she got her job, but her employers said they would work with her.

"I was pleased to get a job," Judy told me, "but I was soon bored silly. The phone didn't ring that much with only four lines. So I just started messing with the computer. I was very careful because I was always afraid I was going to break it.

"I started looking through the My Documents file and the MS Office® documents. I noticed how to go from folder to folder. Then I would forget what I did and have to start all over again."

Finally Judy graduated to Excel®; that was her biggest challenge. Judy thought she was brain dead in math because her dad called her stupid when he tried to explain math to her. As a child Judy didn't understand the way he'd explain it so she had an aversion to math all her life.

"When you get older, it's hard to break these lies that you've told yourself all your life," Judy admitted. "Still, I decided to try to teach myself Excel®. I went through the steps of having the computer add and subtract and do formulas. I also decided to take a night class through community education."

Then Judy decided to try to do the company's service bulletins, documents that provide authority to manufacturers to implement the latest update to the engine. For instance, with a bearing, the service bulletin tells the amount of cycles it can go and when it needs to be changed, depending on the type and size of the turbine engine.

"I asked my boss to show me how to get into the Access® program," Judy said. "Once I showed interest, the company had a technician come in and train me."

That was really data entry. Judy would type the bulletins into an Access® program so that these facts could be recorded. Every time the engine came in, mechanics would refer to this database to determine the service that was needed.

"I never thought I would like anything mechanical," Judy said. "I know that engine well on paper, although I can't go back to the shop and identify the individual parts."

Once Judy learned to type the service bulletins, she became interested in the other areas that interfaced with them. For instance, each service bulletin is linked to a huge database of engine part numbers, specific to each engine. She learned how to update these links and how they interacted.

"I have to admit, I bugged people constantly," Judy said. "I showed so much interest that the sales manager, who is very patient and a born teacher began explaining engines to me. Soon I was doing the whole logbook endorsement document, which is a legal document used to keep track of all the traceable parts on the engine and what work was completed at that event—plus the traceability, which is used to record all the times and cycles on the components."

Learning that was a hair-puller, Judy admitted. "But once I got it, I got it.

"Now they've got me doing accounting and time cards, of all things. It's called an AS400 program, and all those old lies came back when I started learning this: You can't do this. This is math. Just give up and quit. Those tapes really don't ever go away, I guess."

Yet the more Judy would hear those words, the more she'd just grit her teeth and determine to keep going. "Now I know those are lies. And I'm not going back into that old depression. You can see how the Woman of God class changed my life and the church continues to be a real support for me."

Judy has gotten great yearly reviews and her boss says that she is very "efficient." She is a living example of the proverb: "Diligent hands will rule, but laziness ends in slave labor" (Prov. 12:24 NIV). And Solomon's advice that "a person can do nothing better than to . . . find satisfaction in their work" (Eccl. 2:24).

How about you? The apostle Paul advised the early Christians, "But let each one examine his own work, and then he will have rejoicing in himself alone" (Gal. 6:4). What is your attitude toward work? Check the statements below that apply to you:

_____ I try to do my best.

_____ I am conscientious about my work.

_____ I do what is necessary, but I never go further.

_____ I work "heartily."

_____ I talk to friends on the telephone when I'm not busy.

_____ I try to expand my knowledge so that I can do a good job.

If you checked every statement but three and five, you are a good representative of Christ, either in your home or in outside employment. The Lord calls us to walk the life of a transformed person in the workplace, knowing that we are a light drawing others to Christ and a reflection of His love. The apostle Paul advised, "Be diligent to present yourself approved to God, a worker who does not need to be ashamed, rightly dividing the word of truth" (2 Tim. 2:15).

But let me remind you: You must maintain a proper balance here. Your job should not become your god. Even though I work as chief of staff at John Hagee Television Ministries, I always try to keep my priorities straight: God first; my husband, second; my children next; and then my job.

A Christian's second attitude toward work is perseverance.

PERSEVERANCE

Scripture advocates perseverance: "And let us not grow weary" (Gal. 6:9). One woman who showed real persistence was Christine who attended the second Woman of God class.

If a woman has perfect attendance, we award her with a gift book. After graduation Christine came to me and asked me to sign her book. "Mrs. Hagee," she said, "I was here with perfect attendance."

I answered a quick "Yes, Christine, I can see that." And I patronizingly added, "I'm so glad you were able to attend every class."

"Yes, Mrs. Hagee," she said. "That was very difficult for me."

I sighed as I thought to myself, *Yeah, right. The soccer kids were late to practice. Or you were too tired to feel like coming or something like that.*

"I know you don't have much time, but let me tell you my story."

We sat in a back pew of the church and Christine showed me how wrong I'd been. Tears welled in my eyes as I heard her story and repented for what I had thought.

The night of the first session her husband, who was abusive, beat her up at home and then drove her and the children to the church parking lot where he dumped her out of the car. He said, "You're not coming home. You find your own place. You're locked out of the house."

Somehow Christine managed to compose herself and take the children into our day care center. Then she came to class. That evening she asked for a ride to the battered women's shelter.

From then on she either scrounged around for cab fare or got a ride from someone in the class. But she never told anyone what had occurred. It took her five or six sessions before she found a permanent residence for her and her children.

As Christine was talking, tears continued to flow from my eyes, and I began praying silently, *Oh, Jesus, forgive me. Please, never allow me to take someone's attendance or commitment for granted again.*

Christine had the perseverance to attend *every* class, despite these horrific circumstances. And the Woman of God sessions gave her the courage to withstand going back to that abusive situation. Now she's taking in foster children. One Sunday she brought them to visitor's fellowship and asked pastor to pray a prayer of blessing over them.

How about you? Do you persevere when your work becomes difficult? If so, how are you able to do so? Write some ways in the space below:

_____

_____

Both hard work and perseverance will be rewarded, Scripture says. The description of the Proverbs 31 woman ends with the words: "Give her the reward she has earned, and let her works bring her praise at the city gate" (v. 31 NIV). And Proverbs also testifies to the benefit of our work: "In all labor there is profit" (Prov. 14:23). Work is supposed to yield a positive result, including our personal satisfaction and ultimately God's blessing.

> "Now it shall come to pass, if you diligently obey the voice of the Lord your God, to observe carefully all His commandments which I command you today, that the Lord your God will set you high above all nations of the earth.
>
> "And all these blessings shall come upon you and overtake you, because you obey the voice of the LORD your God . . .
>
> "Blessed shall you be when you come in, and blessed shall you be when you go out."
>
> —DEUTERONOMY 28:1–2, 6

chapter seven

Women and Their Relationships:

A Godly Heritage

"Fulfill my joy by being likeminded, having the same love, being of one accord, of one mind."

–PHILIPPIANS 2:2

*Y*ou will remember Moriah Weaver, an eighteen-year-old girl who took the first Woman of God class. Afterward she made a change in her life that impacted her future. "I had always wanted to make a list of what I wanted in a husband," Moriah said. "But after that first class I started changing my perception of what I really wanted. In the Women and Courtship session, Sandy Farhart talked about what to look for in a husband. At the time I wanted to marry someone who looked like Troy Aikmann of the Dallas Cowboys. My mom used to joke about the type of man I was looking for: a handsome man, a rich man, a strong man. After the class I began thinking about what was God's best for me.

"I knew I was growing into a young lady who was looking for 'mister right.' I also knew that marriage is a decision I didn't want to be wrong about. So I sat down and began writing my list. I wanted my husband . . . .

- To love me second only to Christ.
- To be a man of integrity, of character, of high moral standards.
- To be accountable to men in the church.
- To serve in the church.
- To pray with me and read the Bible.

"When my mom looked at this list she was shocked. There was no mention of the man's outward appearance or his wealth. Instead this was a list of characteristics and qualities. And God far surpassed my expectations when He brought Jesse Flores into my life. The Lord knew me better than I did and He knew the man I would marry better than I did. I wanted to marry a man who would respect me second only to Christ, who would honor me and love me. And Jesse always has. Even before he asked me for a date, he asked my parents if it was okay. Talk about respect!

"I also wanted a man who served in the kingdom of God, not someone who just came to church on Sunday and lived like a heathen the rest of the week. Jesse volunteers as the Deputy Director of the Security Ministry at Cornerstone. In everything he does, he truly 'walks the walk.' He never leaves home without our saying this blessing together: 'I love you. God bless you and protect you and give His angels charge over you. I plead the blood of Jesus over you. I pray you have favor with God and man. I break any curses or curse words of assignment against you. In Jesus' name. Amen.'"

As I talked to Moriah I realized how graciously the Lord had honored my prayer to minister to the women in the Woman of God class and to show them His plans for them as His beloved daughters. Jesse and Moriah were going to pass on a godly heritage to their family; they would be blessed by God and bless each other. To me, a godly heritage includes the biblical provision of the blessing.

THE BIBLICAL BLESSING

You might be familiar with the story of Isaac blessing his sons in the Bible. In this chapter I'd like to talk about the power of blessing those closest to us: our spouses and our children. I define the word *blessing* as "releasing the supernatural power of God into another person's life by the spoken word of spiritual authority."

Let's look at the first instance of a father blessing his sons in the Bible. Isaac had twin sons: Esau and Jacob. They were twins, but the biblical description of them doesn't show them resembling one another. I picture Esau as a hairy "mountain of a man," an outdoorsman who loved to hunt. Jacob seems to be a man of moderate stature, a fine-featured and clean-shaven lad, a sensitive thinker.

Esau was born first, but Jacob is said to have taken hold of his brother's heel to try to yank him back from the birth canal. And in their childhood these twins constantly competed with one another, particularly over the birthright, which rewarded the first born with headship over the family and a double amount of inheritance.

This bickering turned into a battle when their father, Isaac, was about 100 years old. At that time the partially blind patriarch was ready to bestow his blessing on his sons. Esau deserved the primary blessing as the firstborn, but Jacob and his mother, Rebekah, plotted to depose him. Jacob dressed in Esau's clothes, and Rebekah fastened goatskin on her son's hands and the smooth part of his neck so he would feel like Esau.

This deception fooled the nearly blind Isaac. Even though he thought he heard Jacob's voice, the old patriarch was deceived by the smell of Esau's clothes and the feel of the hairy, goatskin hands. So Isaac gave Jacob the firstborn's blessing. "May God give you of the dew of heaven, of the fatness of the earth, and plenty of grain and wine. Let peoples serve you, and nations bow down to you. Be master over your brethren, and let your mother's sons bow down to you.

Cursed be everyone who curses you, and blessed be those who bless you!" (Gen. 27:28–29).

In the Bible such a blessing has great power. The blessing, once spoken, cannot be reversed, and this blessing will become a reality.

THE BLESSING, ONCE SPOKEN, CANNOT BE REVERSED

When Esau arrived to receive his rightful blessing as the firstborn, he learned that his deceptive brother had usurped his blessing. Understandably distraught Esau cried, "Have you not reserved a blessing for me? . . . Bless me, even me also, O my father!"

But Isaac told Esau, "I blessed him [Jacob] with an irrevocable blessing" (Gen. 27:33 NLT). Even though Esau was Isaac's favorite son, Isaac could not revoke Jacob's blessing. Still he gave Esau a blessing: "Behold, your dwelling shall be of the fatness of the earth, and of the dew of heaven from above. By your sword you shall live, and you shall serve your brother. And it shall come to pass, when you become restless, that you shall break his yoke from your neck" (Gen. 27:39–40).

Notice that Isaac referred to the blessing he had given to Jacob. He told Esau, "You shall serve your brother." As the patriarch of the family Isaac blessed both Jacob and Esau, but he could not reverse the blessing he had given to Jacob.

Isaac blessed Jacob and Esau—and both blessings became reality.

THE BLESSING, ONCE SPOKEN, BECOMES REALITY!

Christians today often refer to God as "the God of Abraham, Isaac, and *Jacob*." These three patriarchs are the most significant people in the Old Testament. God changed Jacob's name to Israel, and all Hebrew people are his descendents. Jacob heard the Lord predict this when Jacob saw the vision of a ladder reaching up to heaven. God told him:

"I am the LORD God of Abraham your father and the God of Isaac; the land on which you lie I will give to you and your descendants. Also your descendants shall be as the dust of the earth; you shall spread abroad to the west and the east, to the north and the south; and in you and in your seed all the families of the earth shall be blessed. Behold, I am with you and will keep you wherever you go, and will bring you back to this land; for I will not leave you until I have done what I have spoken to you" (Gen. 28:13–15).

This promise—God's blessing—and Isaac's earlier blessing became realities. Jacob's twelve sons form the twelve tribes of Israel. And the Jewish people have spread worldwide from far east to west, from north to south.

Isaac's blessing of Esau was also fulfilled. Esau is referred to as "the father of the Edomites," and he became a wealthy man. Twenty years later when Jacob returned to his homeland he encountered Esau. Fearing his older brother who had threatened to kill him, Jacob sent ahead an abundant gift of many cattle, goats, camels, donkeys, and sheep, quite a procession, I imagine. But at first Esau refused to accept this gift. He said, "I have enough, my brother; keep what you have for yourself" (Gen. 33:9).

Esau had flourished as Isaac's blessing indicated: his dwelling was "of the fatness of the earth." And Esau had broken his brother's yoke from his neck by forgiving Jacob. Esau did finally accept this menagerie of animals and even offered to escort his brother through the land of Seir (Edom) to protect him.

Fortunately the gift of the blessing is not limited to biblical times. This gift is an essential part of everyone's life.

THE GIFT OF THE BLESSING

In Gary Smalley and John Trent's book *The Blessing,* they maintain that all of us yearn for our father's blessing. They suggest five basic ways to give the blessing to a child, a spouse, or a friend. The blessing, they say, includes:

- Meaningful Touch
- A Spoken Message
- Attaching "High Value" to the One Being Blessed
- Picturing a Special Future for the One Being Blessed
- An Active Commitment to Fulfill the Blessing.[1]

Every time my husband and I ask the congregation, "How many of you want your children to live under the blessing of God?" every hand raises. We go on to say, "Do you want your children to be blessed in their health and in their emotions? Do you want them to live with total confidence and a sense of purpose?" Again the entire congregation responds with a fervent "Yes!"

I believe that these five basic parts of the blessing are essential for our children and our spouses. Let's look at how we can express them to our loved ones.

1. Meaningful Touch

Smalley and Trent say, "Meaningful touch was an essential element in bestowing the blessing in Old Testament homes. . . . Each time the blessing was given in the Scriptures, meaningful touching provided a caring background to the words that would be spoken. Kissing, hugging, or the laying on of hands were all a part of bestowing the blessing."[2]

How about you? How could you bless your child with meaningful touch? List some ways in the space below:

_____

_____

_____

Has your touch been the opposite? Have you been so caught up in the stress of raising your children (for instance, alone as a single mother) that most of your "touching" has been in the form of some sort of rebuke, whether deserved or not? If so, note these incidents briefly in the space below:

_____

_____

_____

Our Lord gives us the gift of new beginnings. Say a prayer of repentance and ask the Lord to help you begin anew with your children:

Heavenly Father, I ask that You forgive me for the number of times I have struck my children out of frustration. Even when they have deserved rebuke I have failed to show them love after my reprimand. I have failed to show them I love them by blessing my children with a loving touch. Heal me from the generational curses that have failed to show love and blessings within my own family. Help me to receive my own blessings that You have so freely and lovingly provided. I want to begin anew. In Jesus' name. Amen.

What about your husband? How can you express the blessing to him?

Many women seem to think that men don't want romance in their marriages as much as we women do. Could this thought be one of Satan's ploys to destroy our marriages and our lives through passivity? Definitely. But we also accept this lie for other reasons.

Some of us never had a clear definition of romance in any relationship. We never saw our moms and dads kiss or hug so we don't know how to reproduce that relationship in marriage. Our only point of reference may be a movie or what our friends said when they were talking about their romantic encounters.

Other women's ideas of romance are warped by sexual molestation or a divorce so they don't want to get near a man. The scars are too deep. These women must receive God's healing before they can desire a relationship with a man again.

How about you? What could be holding you back from blessing your husband through touch? Note those thoughts in the space below:

_____

_____

Men need touch as much as women. I often hear women sadly recount how their marriages displayed no warmth, yet when their husbands found new romance with another woman, he lovingly showed them affection. We as wives often fail to notice our husband's equal need for approval through touch.

In the book *What Every Man Wants in a Woman, What Every Woman Wants in a Man,* which my husband and I wrote together, I give seven ways to romance your husband. The power of the touch is one of those ways. It is very important to show affection to your husband every opportunity you get. Take his hand when you are walking together or pat his shoulder as you pass by him. Kiss him often. Even if this hasn't been part of your past behavior, try beginning anew by giving him what you want in return.

Note the ways that you might bless your husband in the space below and then apply them in the days ahead.

_____

_____

2. A Spoken Message

Unfortunately, some parents believe that simply being present for their children communicates a blessing. "Nothing could be further from the truth," Smalley and Trent say. "A blessing becomes so only when it is spoken. . . . The major thing silence communicates is confusion. Children who are left to fill in the blanks when it comes to what their parents think about them will often fail the test when it comes to feeling valuable and secure. Spoken words at least give the hearer an indication that he or she is worthy of some attention."[3]

As parents we have the power to speak life or death into the lives of our children. Proverbs 18:21 says, "Death and life are in the power of the tongue." Some parents speak words that create an atmosphere that chokes and poisons their children's spirits. Proverbs also addresses these parents: "Reckless words pierce like a sword, but the tongue of the wise brings healing" (Prov. 12:18 NIV). When you attack your child's self-esteem with negative labels or nicknames—"Fatso!" "Dumbbell!" "Meathead!"—your words become self-fulfilling prophecies. The Bible calls this a curse.

Those parents are toxic parents. Every time they open their mouths, their poisonous words destroy their child's self-confidence. "Oh, I was only teasing" some parents protest.

No, you cursed your child. Instead begin to give them a blessing.

Most of us are familiar with the blessing at the end of Numbers 6: "The LORD bless you and keep you; the LORD make His face shine upon you, and be gracious to you. The LORD lift up His countenance upon you, and give you peace" (Num. 6:23–26).

You might want to start with these familiar words, "The Lord bless you, _____ (name of your child). Then add "May the Lord . . .

- Prosper all you put your hands to,
- Bless you with divine health,
- Protect you day and night,
- Protect your going out and your coming in,

- Protect your relationships, and
- Protect your mind, your emotions, and your spirit.

Take a moment now to write a blessing for your child. If you have more than one child, begin with the oldest. Then in the next week or so, write a blessing for each of your other children in your prayer journal or a spiral notebook. Write the blessing for your firstborn in the space below, using some of the ideas above and also every promise you want manifested in his or her life:

_____

_____

_____

_____

_____

Husbands also need to hear a spoken blessing. I cannot overstate how important it is to let our husbands know that we love them second only to Christ.

Unfortunately some women put their children before their husbands. But how logical is that? These women could end up losing their husbands, and then they have a fragmented home.

I urge you to keep the proper order here: God, first; husband, second; children, third. Our husbands must be our heroes. And we must express this in the way we speak to them every day. The apostle Paul urged the Ephesians. "Let the wife see that she respects her husband" (Eph. 5:33). Psychologists today agree; they say most men long for the respect of their wives. What better way to show our respect than through a written or spoken blessing.

Yet some women speak strident words to their spouses, rather than words of blessing. These women also need to remember Proverbs 12:18: "Reckless words pierce like a sword, but the tongue of the wise brings healing" (Prov. 12:18 NIV). And then apply Proverbs 25:11: "A word fitly spoken is like apples of gold in settings of silver."

If you have spoken harshly to your husband in the past, are you willing to repent and begin to bless him? If so, pray the prayer below:

As a married woman, Lord, I repent. I ask You to forgive me for the unkind and discouraging words I have spoken to my husband. Forgive me for expecting him to make me happy and thereby placing unbearable expectations upon him.

You are my joy and source, Lord. Help me to lift up my husband daily in prayer for if I hunger and thirst after righteousness, I will be satisfied. Father, I thank You for the gift of my husband. Help me to show respect and honor for him. In Jesus' name. Amen.

After praying this prayer, are you ready to bless your husband? If so, add to this blessing:

Father, I pray that You would bless my husband, enlarge his territory, keep Your hand upon him, and keep him from evil that he will cause no harm. . . .

_____

_____

_____

If you are unable to write a blessing at this time because you feel that your marriage isn't going well, you might want to take a moment to make a list of God's faithfulness in your life. Note such moments in the space below:

_____

_____

Then list the moments you and your husband have shared together, your history as a couple, like the birth of your child or special moments in your relationship:

_____

_____

_____

_____

_____

Are you now better able to bless your husband? Remember, when God created Adam and Eve, the first thing He did was to bless them. "Be fruitful and multiply," He said. "Fill the earth and subdue it; have dominion over the fish of the sea, over the birds of the air, and over every living thing that moves on the earth" (Gen. 1:28). Adam and Eve had a perfect marriage. As my husband says, "Adam didn't have to hear about all the boys Eve could have married. Eve didn't have to hear about how great a cook Adam's mother was. They had no problems with questions like 'Whose house are we going to for the holidays?' Or 'What gifts are we buying for relatives we haven't even seen for a year?'"

But Adam and Eve left the Garden of Eden, and each of us lives in this imperfect world, outside of paradise. Even as daughters of the King we are not perfect and neither are our spouses.

If you didn't write a blessing before, try to write one now. If you did write one, you might want to write another one. Some of us have given our husbands several notes of blessing. And we have also prayed a blessing over them as they lay sleeping. I pray a blessing over my husband every day as he leaves our home. Write a blessing in the space on the following page:

_____

_____

_____

_____

_____

3. Attaching "High Value" to the One Being Blessed

"To value something means to attach honor to it," say Smalley and Trent. "In fact, this is the meaning of the verb 'to bless.' In Hebrew, the word _bless_ literally means 'to bow the knee.' This word was used in showing reverence, even awe, to an important person. . . . Words of blessing should carry with them the recognition that this person is valuable and has redeeming qualities. In the Scriptures, recognition is based on who they are, not simply on their performance."[4]

Think about your children. What are their attributes and talents? List them in the space below:

_____

_____

_____

_____

_____

Now think about your husband. What are his attributes and talents? List them in the space below:

_____

_____

_____

_____

_____

I suggest that you do everything you can to help your husband and your children express these talents in their everyday lives.

Meaningful touch, a spoken message, attaching "high value" to the one being blessed are all ways to give the blessing to someone you love. The fourth way is . . .

4. Picturing a Special Future

Isaac pictured a special future for Jacob: "Let peoples serve you, and nations bow down to you. Be master over your brethren, and let your mother's sons bow down to you" (Gen. 27:29).

Smalley and Trent note that Isaac's words "carried with them the weight of biblical prophecy." Then the authors admit that "as parents or loved ones today, we cannot predict another person's future with biblical accuracy. We can, however, encourage and help them to set meaningful goals. We can also convey to them that the gifts and character traits they have right now are attributes that God can bless and use in the future."[6]

At Cornerstone Church we make proclamations when my husband completes a teaching on healing or restoration. These proclamations foresee a future in which a person will be healed or changed. _The American Heritage Dictionary_ defines the word _proclamation_ as "Something proclaimed, especially an official public announcement."[7] And one of the definitions of the word _proclaim_ is "to praise, extol."[8] I believe a proclamation can be a fact or a part of life.

However, spiritually the words of a proclamation do not have to be operative in our lives at the time we speak them. Instead a proclamation may be an action that I hope and pray will be part of my life in the future—or the life of someone I love. Paul told the early Christians that God "gives life to the dead and calls those things which do not exist as though they did" (Rom. 4:17). Some proclamations at Cornerstone Church invoke God's promise to call our hopes into being.

Write a proclamation for your firstborn in the space below. Then write proclamations for any other children in your prayer journal during the next week:

Lord, I praise You that You have entrusted me with the blessing of _____.
I know that he (she) is . . .

_____

_____

_____

Then write a proclamation for your husband in the space below. You might begin in this way. . . .

Lord, I acknowledge that my husband is the priest of my home. I praise You that he seeks first the
kingdom of God and Your righteousness, and that everything will be added to him. . . .

_____

_____

_____

The final way to bless a loved one is by committing your support to that person.

5. An Active Commitment

This last element of the blessing pictures the responsibility that goes with giving the blessing, Smalley and Trent say, "Parents today, in particular, need to rely on the Lord to give them the strength and staying power to confirm their children's blessing." They have God's Word through Scriptures as a guide, the authors say, plus the power of the indwelling Holy Spirit.[9]

Think about the ways you can give your child the support he or she needs to fulfill his or her blessing. Write those ways in the space below:

_____

_____

_____

_____

Now think about how you can support your husband. After that first Woman of God class, Moriah Flores also wrote a list of the changes she needed to make to support her future husband. Moriah told me, "So many women say, 'I want this or that in a husband.' When they do, I think, *Who are you? If you get hooked up with this wonderful guy you might drag him down and make him an average Joe because you are unequally yoking him.* I realized that if I wanted this great, incredible, amazing guy, I needed to be a great, incredible, amazing woman. I wanted to be this man's dream woman, just as I wanted him to be my dream man. I realized I needed to change.

"If I wanted my husband to read the Bible with me, I needed to be in the habit of reading the Bible. If I wanted him to pray with me, I needed to spend time praying and seeking the Lord. I also knew I needed to be more organized and to learn to budget my money so I wouldn't be a burden to my future husband."

Can you think of some changes that you need to make in order to support your husband? List those changes in the space below:

_____

_____

Are there some other ways that you can support your husband? Write those ways in the space below:

_____

_____

_____

Some of you might only think of how you can support your husband in his work. Let me add that a little romance is one of the greatest supports you can give your spouse. For instance, when my husband comes home in the evening, he walks into the kitchen, gives me a hug and a kiss, and asks how my day went. Then he goes into his study and drops off his briefcase, which is filled with research for Sunday's sermon or the latest book he is writing. From there he goes into our bedroom and watches the evening news until dinner is ready.

If, when he comes through the door, I tell him that he can't go into our bedroom because I have something special planned, he immediately smiles and usually says, "Awww!" no matter how tough his day has been. The mood has been set.

When I call him to dinner, he walks into our bedroom with anticipation and sees a small table set with linen and china in front of the fireplace. There are candles on the table and a single red rose in a crystal vase. He loves red. The only light in the room comes from the lit candles and the fire. I then serve a five-course dinner.

Men like to be pampered. The blessing they receive usually lasts into the next day—and even the day after that!

Let me end this chapter by proclaiming that you will foster a godly heritage in your family so each of you will receive all that God has for you.

The LORD bless you, and keep you;

The LORD make His face shine upon you, and be gracious to you;

The LORD lift up His countenance upon you, and give you peace.

—NUMBERS 6:24–27

chapter eight

And God Said, . . . "Let There Be Sex":

Intimate and Unashamed

"All things are lawful for me, but all things are not helpful. All things are lawful for me, but I will not be brought under the power of any."
—I CORINTHIANS 6:12

*I*n the Woman of God seminars, Dr. Scott Farhart, my brother-in-law, speaks to the women about sex. Dr. Farhart is an obstetrician in San Antonio and was elected chairman of the Department of Obstetrics and Gynecology at Northeast Methodist Hospital in 1991 and elected chief of staff of that hospital in 1995 at the age of thirty-five, the youngest chief of staff in San Antonio history. Scott has also written a book about sexuality, *Intimate and Unashamed*, which I highly recommend.

I am asking him to write this chapter of the workbook, just as he wrote this chapter in *The King's Daughter*.

A SEXUAL UPDATE BY DR. SCOTT FARHART

Unfortunately the church is beginning to mirror the secular world in the incidences of STDs. We have opened this door by not teaching our young women and men about the godly purpose of sex. Instead they have learned about sex from their friends, television, and movies. In this chapter I want to give Christians a clear vision of the threat of STDs. We are going to concentrate on three sexually transmitted diseases (STDs): Chlamydia, herpes, and HIV.

The prevalence of STDs in this country has been so profound and so destructive that a colleague of mine, Dr. Joe McIhaney, Jr., left his practice over nine years ago after he founded The Medical Institute for Sexual Health, which disseminates information about the different sexual diseases. His decision was sparked by the consequences of Chlamydia: "The pain I saw in the lives of so many couples motivated me to dedicate the rest of my professional career to educating people about this and other health problems associated with risky sexual behavior."[1]

Just as Dr. McIlhaney, I have seen many marriages struggle under the pain of different sexual diseases. STDs bring tremendous feelings of guilt, shame, anger, violation, and betrayal. The once joyous act of intercourse now carries a heavy price tag that some may pay for a lifetime.

I see cases of STDs in my private practice almost every day. They shatter the fantasy world so many people live in when it comes to sexual activity. No one in television or movies, romance novels or contemporary music, seems to pay a price for their sexual conduct. So I guess it should not surprise me that the average person is in shock when he or she is given the diagnosis of an STD. No one prepared this person for the real world as it exists today—a world where sexually transmitted diseases run rampant.

Sexually transmitted diseases can be divided into two categories: bacterial and viral. STDs that are bacterial can be cured with antibiotics; those that are viral have no cure at the present time.

One of the most common bacterial STDs is Chlamydia.

CHLAMYDIA

This sexual disease is most common in teenage girls because the cervix of young women is covered with ectropion (an immature tissue that is vulnerable to infection). If you are the mother or sister of a young girl, you need to educate her about this disease. Dr. McIlhaney left his practice because he "began to realize that most of my patients had never been told about the enormous threat this disease can be to their future fertility. Many of these women may never have their own biological child."[2]

And this is also true of adult women. The Chlamydia infection can travel from the vagina to infect, scar, and damage the ovaries, the fallopian tubes, other organs, and the lining of the abdominal cavity. This is known as pelvic inflammatory disease (PID) and up to 40 percent of women with Chlamydia will develop PID.

Once the fallopian tubes are infected, the healthy egg is either damaged or can become lodged inside a fallopian tube where it can be fertilized and grow, causing an ectopic or tubal pregnancy. Since the fallopian tube cannot stretch as the baby grows, the tube can rupture and cause massive internal bleeding.

Even if a woman with Chlamydia can successfully have a baby, she will have pelvic pain that can interfere with intercourse and normal activities for quite a few years.

Unfortunately many women do not realize they have Chlamydia because they do not have any symptoms. However, when symptoms do occur, they include an abnormal genital discharge from the vagina and/or painful urination. These symptoms are usually mild, but they sometimes develop into abdominal pain, high fever, and even shock.

Anyone with such symptoms needs to seek medical treatment immediately. Several antibiotics can treat Chlamydia, and early treatment can prevent PID and infertility.

One of the most common viral STDs is herpes.

HERPES

Two types of herpes simplex virus have been identified: herpes simplex type 1 (HSV-1) and herpes simplex type 2 (HSV-2). Type 1 has traditionally been called oral herpes and is associated with lesions around the mouth called cold sores. This form of herpes is not typically thought of as a sexually transmitted disease. Most sexual herpes occur from HSV-2, which causes blisters in the genital region about six days after exposure to an infected person.

Common symptoms include a burning or itching pain at the site of the infection, which often begins before any blisters are visible. A week after the blisters appear, they rupture to form "wet" ulcers. If this is the first infection, these blisters will usually begin to heal a week later and then become covered with a scab. The person can also experience general symptoms like fever, headache, and muscle aches. The complete cycle of pain, blister formation, ulceration, and healing typically lasts about three weeks.[3]

During the first occurrence the virus migrates from the nerve ending in the infected area along the course of the nerve to the dorsal root ganglia located near the spinal cord.[4] Once there, the virus becomes temporarily inactive and can remain latent for the remainder of the infected person's life.[5] However, nearly everyone will have at least one recurrence of this disease and most will experience periodic recurrences for several years (if not for life).[6]

Though many women believe a Pap smear will detect herpes, this is not normally so. Most often herpes is diagnosed from the detection of abnormal cells, viral antigens, or viral DNA from a suspicious skin lesion. Unfortunately antiviral medications do not cure herpes; however, they can decrease the frequency, duration, and severity of the symptoms.

As I said in my book, *Intimate and Unashamed*, long after the herpes lesions have cleared, the emotional and psychological stress remains. I see many women in my office for whom the diagnosis of herpes hangs like a scarlet letter around their necks. They wonder if they are obligated to disclose this history to future sexual partners and if this knowledge will hinder that new relationship. Once married, they bear the burden of preventing transmission to their newborns and struggle to explain why a cesarean section is needed while trying to hide their secret shame.

The viral STD that receives the most publicity is Human Immunodeficiency Virus (HIV), the agent responsible for AIDS.

AIDS

This disease is transmitted by exposure to infected blood or other body fluids, like semen and vaginal secretions. The symptoms include the typical tiredness, aching, nausea, and fever associated with the flu. Once these initial symptoms fade, there are usually no recognizable symptoms for about ten years, although new treatments may further delay the onset.

Within a few years after the AIDS onset, patients usually die of such diseases as tuberculosis, pneumocystis pneumonia, certain types of fungal and yeast infections, and persistent and unusual intestinal infections. AIDS patients also experience high rates of cancer, including lymphomas and Kaposi's sarcoma. In the United States alone, AIDS is the leading cause of death for people between the ages of twenty-five and forty-four, despite the best advances of modern medicine.

All of these facts about STDs are significant, but they don't fully portray a woman's suffering when she is afflicted with these diseases. Unfortunately LaGena Lookabill Greene knows this pain.

LaGena was raised in a loving Christian family in Charlotte, North Carolina. She attended college on an academic scholarship and after graduating with honors, she was selected as Miss Hawaiian Tropic USA. She spent the next year traveling around the world, attending events like the Cannes Film Festival and being photographed on exotic tropical islands for ads in magazines such as *Glamour, Cosmopolitan,* and *People.*

When her responsibilities to Hawaiian Tropic were complete, LaGena moved to Los Angeles where she spent the next three years working as a television and film actress. Before she went to Hollywood, she promised her father to never compromise her morals off screen in order to get a role onscreen. And she kept that vow. She also rejected roles that she found to be questionable. She avoided drugs and alcohol and stayed away from the Hollywood party scene.

By the age of twenty-five her acting career was soaring. In just three years she guest-starred on twenty-five primetime television shows, co-starred in five feature films, and worked in numerous commercials and music videos. But a decision she made the same year changed her life forever.

LaGena had been dating Daniel Joseph Greene, an actor she met when they appeared in a movie together. They fell in love, and she was certain Danny was the man she would marry. Then Danny was cast in a nighttime series, *Falcon Crest*, and his character became very popular. LaGena says, "Hollywood is like a big 'candy store' and unfortunately Danny had a 'sweet tooth.' More than once I caught Danny with his hands in the 'cookie jar' so I broke up with him. I soon got a part in *Born to Race*, a movie that would be filmed in my hometown of Charlotte."

While LaGena was in Charlotte, Tim Richmond, an old friend, began pursuing her romantically. He was good-looking, funny, and a successful NASCAR driver. He told her he loved her, wanted to marry her, and wanted to have children. That's just what LaGena longed to hear. "I had always planned to be married around age twenty-seven and have my first child by thirty, my second child a few years later."

LaGena resisted his proposals until September 10, 1986 when she accompanied him to Baltimore where *USA Today* wanted to interview NASCAR's hottest new driver. After the interview Tim suggested that they fly to New York for the afternoon, and then have dinner. In the romantic environment of a posh hotel overlooking Central Park, Tim asked her to marry him. They had been dating for several months and he had already asked her to marry him two times before.

Finally LaGena agreed, and she gave in to his sexual advances. After they had consummated their relationship, Tim seemed angry and argumentative. LaGena left New York and flew back to Charlotte. They were supposed to spend Thanksgiving together in Los Angeles, but he never appeared and never called to tell her why. She never saw Tim again.

Several weeks later a sports agent called with a rumor that Tim was sick with AIDS. LaGena thought this was a vicious rumor, but when she hung up the phone she called her gynecologist. He told her that women didn't get AIDS. At that time AIDS was actually know as GRID, Gay-Related Immune Disorder.

Still LaGena asked her doctor to test her anyway. The results were negative, just as the doctor expected. At the time no one realized that there could be a window of about three months between the time of infection and a positive test. But within the next two weeks, LaGena became very sick with what was diagnosed as "a bad case of the flu." This flu-like illness was really seroconversion illness, a time when the blood converts to positive for HIV.

Soon after she recovered from the illness, LaGena received another disturbing phone call, this time from a *USA Today* reporter who wanted her to confirm a rumor that Tim Richmond was dying from AIDS in a hospital in Cleveland, Ohio. This rumor led LaGena to ask her doctor for another test, even though she was not really worried that she had the illness. After all, she had previously tested negative, and AIDS victims were emaciated gay men with gaunt faces and hollow eyes. She was a muscular, energetic young woman.

A week after the test, her gynecologist called on the telephone. "Are you sitting down?" he asked. LaGena could hear the tremor in his voice. She almost anticipated his next words: "Your test came back positive."

The obvious next question was the most difficult: "How long do I have to live?" "Probably two years."

LaGena now knew why her boyfriend was in hiding. He had kept a dreadful secret from her and by doing so had given her a terminal, dreadful disease.

"Never before had there been a problem I could not solve with my own resources," LaGena told me. "At first I was numb and did not eat or sleep for a week. I was overwhelmed with a flood of thoughts and emotions. I certainly felt guilty for ruining my life when my parents had sacrificed their whole lives to give me a privileged, comfortable, happy life. They had taught me good values and now I would let them down. I knew they would be devastated."

The same week LaGena tested positive she read that 51 percent of Americans thought people with AIDS should be quarantined on an island. She heard about pools that were closed because a person with AIDS had gone swimming. She saw a horrifying report on television about two young boys who had contracted AIDS from blood transfusions. Other parents did not want these boys attending school with their children so they shattered the windows of the boys' home with bullets and attempted to burn down their house. Hysteria about AIDS was everywhere. This disease was the leprosy of the twentieth century, and its victims were modern-day lepers.

All of LaGena's studying and scholarships now meant nothing. Neither did the success in her acting career. She was going to die and leave behind a legacy of shame and disgrace. At twenty-six years old, her dreams were shattered.

"I was petrified and saw no escape except immediate death," LaGena said. "I wanted my suicide to look like an accident. Skydiving was a hobby so I decided to jump out of an airplane over the Mojave Desert in California and not pull the rip cord. However, as I fell from the plane tears flowed from my eyes as I thought of my parents and brother. I would never see them again. I was free-falling at 200 feet per second. I had been taught to pull the ripcord at 5,000 feet. When my altimeter registered 4,500 feet, I looked at the target on the ground where my bones would be crushed in the dust. Now my altimeter registered 4,000 feet. Then 3,500 feet.

"Suddenly a Great Presence, not an audible voice exactly, but a loving and commanding voice, said, 'LaGena, you want to live.' I truly believe this was the voice of God. I quickly reached for my ripcord, which had twisted around to a place I could barely reach. I found it. I pulled hard and finally landed safely on the ground."

At first LaGena didn't tell anyone about her illness. Then one night, all alone in the darkness of her bedroom, LaGena cried out in desperation to God and asked Him to help her. She decided to confide in her former boyfriend, Danny Greene. They had remained friends after their breakup. Her decision proved to be God's answer to her prayer. In the days ahead Danny became like a big brother and coach.

LaGena did not think she could be loved by a man; she considered herself "damaged goods." Then she read 2 Corinthians 5:17: "Therefore, if anyone is in Christ, he is a new creation; old things have passed away." She had rededicated her life to Christ at a service in California in 1987. She was a new creation, beautiful and marvelous in God's sight.

God honored LaGena's desire and blessed her in a way she could never have imagined. On Valentine's Day of 1990, four years after she was infected with AIDS, she and Danny Greene pledged to marry each other "For better or worse, in sickness and in health, till death do us part." Danny is her soul mate, her best friend, her lover, and her confidant.

In the many years of her struggle with AIDS, LaGena has been near death nine times. On one occasion her viral load skyrocketed from being undetectable, which is good, to over one million copies, which is critically dangerous. She went to the emergency room with an overwhelming headache, one much more painful than any previous migraines. A lumbar puncture revealed that her brain was swollen; she had encephalopathy.

"My head literally felt like it was splitting wide open," LaGena said. "My body was on fire with a fever of 105. I was so dehydrated, the nurses tried unsuccessfully seven times to get IV's started. My veins had collapsed.

"For two weeks I was in a painful delirium. My eyes could not open because the light felt like sharp knives."

Perhaps the closest LaGena came to death was when she was "wasting." She was down to eighty-nine pounds. So thin and fragile, the doctor gave her six months to live.

She was hospitalized so she could be hooked up to all kinds of tubes and monitors. As usual Danny was there with her. "I sat on the edge of the bed next to my tiny little LaGena—all I heard were the sounds of her breathing and the IV monitor beeping. My heart was bursting as I thought I was losing her. I was crying as silently as I could and I whispered, 'Dear God, please heal her. Give us more time.'

"LaGena slightly opened her eyes and with tears rolling down her cheeks she said in a soft voice, 'I love you, Bunny. I'm sorry for being such a burden.' Then she went back to sleep.

"I thought of all the sermons we had heard and how God's Word always gave us such peace. At that moment I felt that peace, and I knew it was real. Yet I had never committed my life to Christ. Right then, I needed Him. I couldn't fix this situation. I was so afraid of losing her. I laid my hand on her and said, 'Lord Jesus, I put my precious LaGena in Your hands. I release her to You, Lord. Thy will be done.' Then I prayed the prayer of salvation. I will always have my LaGena to thank for leading me to my Jewish Carpenter, Yeshua, my Lord and Savior. Isn't it odd how so often it's not until we're at the lowest, weakest point that we are finally willing to turn our lives over to Him?"

Danny's prayers, along with those of her family, friends, and church were soon answered. While she was in the hospital a brand new class of drugs became available. With this medication she gained up to 142 pounds in just three months. Her rebound, along with others who cheated death with these new drugs, was called "The Lazarus Effect" by the medical community.

But LaGena will never be well again. She takes sixty pills a day and three shots. These medications have many side effects, which caused her to develop diabetes. For four years straight she vomited and had diarrhea every day. She wore diapers.

She could not walk, sit, laugh, cry, or cough without intense pain. Thankfully she is no longer a prisoner of the bathroom; however, her current medications put her at risk for heart and liver disease.

LaGena was diagnosed with AIDS in 1987. She was given two years to live; instead she has lived over eighteen years through God's grace and love. And she and Danny have shared over fifteen years of marriage. God has blessed them, but LaGena will never recover from AIDS unless some miraculous cure is discovered.

Both LaGena Lookabill Greene and I believe that science is proving what God the Father knew all along. The only way to prevent serious, lifelong disease and death is for both partners to remain abstinent until marriage and then be faithful to one another for life. Abstinence is not some outdated and archaic moral position; it is literally a matter of life and death. LaGena speaks throughout the United States to encourage teenagers and adults to remain sexually pure.

A FINAL WORD

Since beginning A Woman of God we have noticed that at the end of the session devoted to the ravages of sexually transmitted diseases, a number of women will come forward to ask for prayer. Having already contracted a sexually transmitted disease, these women need to know how to resolve their past. Most of these women are not currently involved in risky sexual practices; instead they are wives and mothers who have a past—don't we all!

This is a common scenario that I see in my office. Whether through mistakes the women made, or the disease that was brought to them by an unfaithful spouse, many women feel "damaged." Some sexually transmitted diseases, such as herpes or HIV, stay with you for a lifetime. And while your life may change and your convictions about sexual purity may strengthen, your lingering past haunts the present.

I remember a patient who is also a fellow church member. Early in my practice, she came to my office with a classic case of herpes. She had married a man in the church who had also been married before. I assumed that this current infection was a consequence of her husband unknowingly bringing his past sexual sin into their present relationship. Unfortunately this happens very frequently, when a partner has a past sexual history that includes disease.

But this case was very different. The diagnosis of herpes became the smoking gun the wife was looking for to confirm her suspicions about her husband's unfaithfulness. I had naively assumed that such behavior did not happen in the church, certainly not in my church. As I said, I was young. But as I have continued to care for this woman for more than fifteen years I have learned a valuable lesson. She must live with this infection for the rest of her life. While she may forgive her now ex-husband, it doesn't take away the reality that this wrong remains alive and well in her body.

In any of these situations, whether an STD came to you because of your own poor choices or the sin of an unfaithful spouse or the "innocent" transmission from a previously infected partner, the result is that you feel damaged. For many women, this impacts their sexual self-image and the degree of intimacy they will experience.

Men seem to be able to separate their past sexual history from their present relationships far better than women. A man rarely tells me he feels "unclean" or less sexually attractive because of his sexually transmitted disease. It is merely a fact of life, a hassle that one deals with and moves on. That may be a reflection of the way men deal with issues in general, but the reality is that they seem to be much freer to pursue their marital relationship, despite the lingering disease, than do their female counterparts.

I am privileged to be able to pray with these women and to set them free from their wrong thinking during the Woman of God seminar. A sexually transmitted disease, such as herpes, may stay with you, but the disease does not have control over you and your sexual self-esteem unless you let it. You must separate the physical disease from the emotional and spiritual connection you are making with your husband.

In my twenty years of medical practice I have never heard a husband say that he is less attracted to his wife because she has an occasional herpes outbreak or a recurrence of a genital wart. He just wants to be with his spouse and unite with her as God intended.

If you have contracted an STD, take a moment now to bow your head and receive God's forgiveness. Then write a letter to yourself, forgiving yourself for this mistake of your past. Reread that letter every time you are tempted to accuse yourself again.

If your spouse has given you an STD, you must also take a moment to bow your head and ask God to help you forgive him. Then write a letter to him, telling him that you have done so. If possible, give him this letter. If not, keep it among your valuables so you can reread it every time you are tempted to accuse him again.

I tell the women in the Woman of God seminar, "If God has forgiven you, and your spouse holds no ill-will against you, you are under an obligation to forgive yourself and embrace who you are, the past included. Only then can you attain the level of sexual intimacy that God intended."

LaGena Lookabill Greene says, "Danny and I tell married couples, 'We want to encourage you and your loved one to play together, to pray together, and to live as if you were dying. We have and God has blessed us so abundantly."

For more information about sexually transmitted diseases and abstinence-based education, you can contact The Medical Institute for Sexual Health at 1-800-892-9484 or visit their website at www.medinstitute.org.

I am my beloved's,
And his desire is toward me.

—SONG OF SOLOMON 7:10

chapter nine

The Temple of the Lord:

My Body, a Vessel of Honor

"Do you not know that your body is the temple of the Holy Spirit who is in you?"

—I CORINTHIANS 6:19

$\mathcal{P}$astor Hagee and I met Dr. Don Colbert after my husband read Don's book *What You Don't Know May Be Killing You.* We were impressed with his knowledge and his ability to solve major health problems. Dr. Colbert received his residency training from Florida Hospital in Orlando, Florida, specializing in family medicine, and he is now in private practice in central Florida. He has received extensive training in public health and preventative medicine and is a board-certified family practice physician.

Throughout the Woman of God seminars we ask specialists to speak. Dr. Colbert did a session on health, which will form the basis of this chapter.

DR. COLBERT ON GOD'S PLAN FOR YOUR HEALTH

I'm going to take you through the Scriptures to show you God's plan for our bodies and how we have gotten off course. I believe God is calling us to become living epistles. That's certainly what Scripture indicates.

God revealed His initial plan for us in Genesis 1. He said, "See, I have given you every herb that yields seed which is on the face of all the earth, and every tree whose fruit yields seed; to you it shall be for food. Also, to every beast of the earth, to every bird of the air, and to everything that creeps on the earth, in which there is life, I have given every green herb for food" (vv. 29–30).

The Lord's initial plan was for man and beast to be vegetarians. And this continued throughout history until Noah and his family left the ark. At this time God gave Noah some new instructions. He said, "Every moving thing that lives shall be food for you. I have given you all things, even as the green herbs. But you shall not eat flesh with its life, that is, its blood" (Gen. 9:3–4).

God expanded upon this in Leviticus 11. He said, "These are the animals which you may eat among all the animals that are on the earth. Among the animals, whatever divides the hoof, having cloven hooves and chewing the cud—that you may eat" (vv. 2–3). These were the clean animals, because these animals had less disease. Proper cooking would kill these parasites. But if the animal was improperly cooked, people could get parasites, viruses, and bacteria.

God further delineated man's diet in verse 9: "These you may eat of all that are in the water: whatever in the water has fins and scales, whether in the seas or in the rivers—that you may eat." We could eat fish, but not fish without scales, which omitted shrimp, crab, lobster, and clams. Jesus never ate such food.

I classify foods in two categories: God-made and man-made.

FOOD CLASSIFICATIONS

MAN-MADE FOODS

Unfortunately most of us have been raised on man-made foods. Usually our food preferences are formed by the time we're four or five years old, certainly mine were. I was raised in a southern family with southern home cooking. We ate chicken fried steak. We ate fried pork chops. We ate fried catfish and chicken. And my mom fried many foods in bacon grease. In fact, she kept a cup of bacon grease right on the stove. Each morning when she cooked bacon, she would save the grease in that cup. Then at night she would take a big tablespoon of that grease and put it in the string beans or the broccoli.

Southerners are not the only residents of America who have particular diets. For instance, Texans also have specific food tastes. They love lots of meat, lots of pork, lots of tacos and burritos and quesadillas—and lots of tortilla chips.

All of these tastes were programmed in us and associated with pleasant events like birthday parties and family outings. When we get tired or stressed or depressed, guess what we reach for? These comforting foods from our childhood.

Think about your own childhood. What foods did you enjoy then? List them in the space below:

_____

_____

_____

Do you still enjoy (crave) them now? I bet so.

Yet Jesus wants every one of us to prosper and be in health, even as our soul prospers. Unfortunately, we get in the way. Our flesh craves a food that our mind thinks we need.

When I was working as an extern for a month in Mississippi as a medical student, I noticed many cases of high blood pressure, strokes, and heart attacks. I wondered if there could be a connection between what the Southerners were eating and these diseases. And this proved to be true.

Three types of foods are particularly offensive: fast foods, processed foods, and sugar.

FAST FOODS

The fast food industry is a multibillion-dollar industry that is present on every corner of America. We like fast foods because they are *fast*. But they don't have the vitamins, the minerals, the antioxidants, the phytonutrients (a plant nutrient), and the fiber we need. Instead they contain fat—lots and lots of fat—plus salt and processed carbohydrates that convert to sugar, which causes us to crave these foods.

Think about the last time you saw a particular fast food sign. You can almost smell the food. The children are begging to eat there so you drive through or sit in the small dining room and watch the kids play outside after their Happy Meal®.

How often do you give in to this urge? Note that in the space below:

_____

Could you bypass these restaurants in the future? If so, how? List three ways in the space below:

_____

_____

_____

PROCESSED FOODS

A processed food is a food that was natural until man altered it, taking out most of the vitamins, most of the minerals, and most of the fiber.

In 2001 Phillip Morris began buying the processed food companies. Why? Because these foods are highly addictive. Now this company owns Oreo® cookies, Lifesavers®, Ritz® crackers, and Oscar Meyer® wieners.

Processed food companies hire the best chemists so they can make these foods as addictive as possible. You eat one cookie, you have to have another. Why?

Because these refined foods have a high glycemic index that causes your sugar to go up and you get caught in the sugar cycle of craving these foods. You eat potato chip after potato chip. Cracker after cracker. If you don't eat something every three or four hours, you're going to have a ravenous appetite. You're also going to get irritable and cranky.

These foods generally have hydrogenated fat, the worst possible fat, which raises your cholesterol and causes you to gain tremendous weight. Your joints start breaking down and you get arthritis in your knees, in your hips, in your back. You don't feel good so you don't exercise. And you can't move quickly so the weight piles on faster and faster. It's a vicious cycle. All this sets you up for high blood pressure, Type II diabetes, cardiovascular disease, and eventually cancer.

When patients first come to my office, I often find nutritional deficiencies in minerals, especially magnesium and zinc. About 75 percent of people are low on magnesium, for instance. Many people are low in Vitamin D. I also find deficiencies in Vitamin B. I recommend a good multivitamin and maybe a magnesium supplement.

How many processed foods do you eat? Think about what you've eaten in the last two weeks. Check the processed foods that you've consumed:

_____ White bread

_____ White flour

_____ White rice

_____ Bagels

_____ Pretzels

_____ Donuts

_____ Crackers

_____ Hot dogs

Could you eliminate some of these foods from your diet? If so, how? Write three ways in the space below:

_____

_____

_____

SUGAR

Unfortunately we're a nation of sugar addicts. The average American consumes 11, 250 pounds of sugar during his or her lifetime. That's half a truckload![1]

God intended us to eat sugar in fruit. But we manipulated sugar cane, just as we manipulated processed food. We took the sugar cane and extracted the sugar out of it, and when we did, we omitted the fiber in the cane, which prevented our blood sugar from rising rapidly. This dead food only increases our craving because we're not getting the nutrition we need.

We are trapped in a vicious cycle. We crave sugar. And if we don't get sugar every three or four hours, our blood sugar dips. And we crave even more sugar. We've got to have it. We've got to have it *now*.

Yet sugar raises the hormone insulin. This hormone tells our bodies to store fat, instead of burning it. So when we exercise, we burn sugar (or glucose in the muscle and liver, which is called glycogen) instead. Our fat remains locked inside our fat cells. This makes it very easy to gain weight and extremely difficult to lose weight.

I'll never forget a young woman we'll call Susan. She had two young children in elementary school and also worked as a secretary for a demanding boss. She'd wake up every morning, make the kids breakfast, and get them off to school. Then she would get dressed for work. But before she left, she would clean the kitchen. At work her boss produced a continuous stream of memos, correspondence, and other duties for her. She found it necessary to work straight through lunch so she would ask her fellow workers to bring back some fast food to keep her energy up. She'd also drink soft drinks and eat donuts, anything for that quick energy boost. She'd use sugar and caffeine to overcome her fatigue.

What happened? In three years Susan went from 130 pounds to 200 pounds. She also developed high cholesterol, Type II diabetes, and high blood pressure. When she came to my office she was overweight and exhausted. I asked her about her life. And she revealed that she only got four to six hours of sleep at night.

Are you like Susan? Are you addicted to sugar? Think about the last two weeks. List the sweets that you have eaten in the space below:

_____

_____

_____

Could you eliminate some or all of these foods? List the ones you are willing to eliminate in the space below:

_____

_____

God is calling Susan and all of us to temperance, to exercise restraint and self-control.

TEMPERANCE

Many of us are familiar with the fruits of the Spirit: love, joy, peace, longsuffering, kindness, goodness, faithfulness, gentleness, and self-control (Gal. 5:22–23). But we often forget the last fruit: self-control.

Instead of practicing self-control, we eat so fast, our body doesn't have time to say, "Stop! You're full!" Unfortunately it takes about twenty minutes for our hypothalamus to indicate that we should stop eating. When we only chew sparingly and wash our food down with a Coke or sweet tea, we miss this important signal. Believe it or not, I recommend that you set your fork down and chew your food thirty times.

After the apostle Paul identified the fruits of the Spirit, he told the Galatians: "Those who are Christ's have crucified the flesh with its passions and desires" (Gal. 5:24). He exhorted them, "If we live in the Spirit, let us also walk in the Spirit" (Gal. 5:25).

Believe me, we have not crucified the flesh if we are allowing fast foods, processed foods, and sugar to dominate our diets. Most of the patients who come to me have seen several doctors. Yet they haven't been healed. I tell them, "You have to lay certain foods on the altar."

I also tell them they have to quit frying their food. Why? Because certain fats are deadly fats. Some of the worst foods are deep-fried foods: French fries, fried chicken, fried catfish. These fats are forming tremendous amounts of free radicals that go through your body and damage or begin to destroy cell membranes. When you eat French fries that have been drowned in grease, you're eating the grease.

Carbohydrates are doing the same thing to us when we choose the wrong kind of carbohydrates. When we choose processed foods—white bread, white flour, white rice, bagels, pretzels, donuts, and crackers—they generally raise our blood sugar. We then start on that vicious cycle of low blood sugar, which causes us to crave more sugar or processed foods.

The worst fats are hydrogenated fats, fats found in shortening, most all margarines, commercial peanut butter, cake icing, cookies, candies, and pies.

There's a better choice. Instead we can reach for Ezekiel bread, millet bread, spelt bread, or spelt tortillas. God always gives us a choice. We can choose life or we can choose death. First Corinthians 3:16–17 says, "Do you not know that you are the temple of God and that the Spirit of God dwells in you? If anyone defiles the temple of God, God will destroy him. For the temple of God is holy, which temple you are."

Can you imagine someone in Jesus' days walking into Solomon's temple or Herod's temple with a bagful of trash and throwing that garbage down in the middle of the Holy of Holies? Can you imagine what the people would have done to this person? Probably taken him out and stoned him.

Yet we are trashing God's temple by eating the wrong foods that lead to disease. Instead we need to exercise restraint. We need to say, "I'm going to take control over this. I'm going to take dominion over this processed food, this fast food, this sugar, and over some of the foods from my childhood."

When we do so, our weight starts to come down, our blood pressure comes down, and our cholesterol comes down.

Americans also tend to overeat.

OVEREATING

What causes us to overeat? Often our hormones and our emotions are the triggers.

OUR HORMONES

An imbalance of female hormones sometimes causes women to crave sweets. During their menstrual cycle or right before their period, they'll crave chocolate, for instance, because their hormones are out of balance. Women also crave sweets and carbohydrates when they are pregnant or during menopause. And when their hormones are imbalanced women are usually irritable. Hormones might seem to be the bad guys here, but they can be advantageous if they are balanced properly.

I often use blood or saliva testing to find a patient's current estrogen and progesterone levels. Then I suggest natural hormones, like triple estrogen or biestrogen, to provide balance. I talk about this therapy in my *Bible Cure for Menopause* book.

Women can also balance their hormones and delay or lessen the symptoms of premenopause, which begins in the mid-thirties, by avoiding the following: junk foods, processed foods, alcohol, margarine, sugar, caffeine, and fried foods. Instead, they can select foods that are nutritionally healthy, like fresh fruits, lean meats, fresh vegetables, and whole grains.

OUR EMOTIONS

Often when people try to diet on their own strength, they experience guilt. And when they do, they eat. Depression is also an emotion that will cause us to eat, as does excessive stress, anxiety, and grief. We turn to our comfort foods, often those pleasurable foods from our childhood, to ease our pain. We remember when we attended a birthday party as a child and enjoyed eating ice cream and chocolate cake. We were enjoying ourselves at that party so we now reach for that food to get the same feeling.

Susan, the young woman who went from 130 to 200 pounds, had some emotional issues. She was depressed because she felt her life was a dead-end. She was working from sunup to sundown, and she only got four to six hours of sleep at night.

First I put her on some natural supplements that helped her depression. Then the people in my office took her through forgiveness therapy, and they also addressed the spiritual issues. She was so exhausted by the end of the week that she didn't go to church on Sunday so we had her listen to good Bible-based teaching tapes. We had her read the Bible and some Christian self-help books. We treated her physically, mentally, and spiritually.

Susan asked me to help her lose weight and to prescribe a pill to give her energy. "What about amphetamines? Would they help me?" she asked.

A lot of patients ask for such a quick fix. Diet pills can be successful at first. They raise your metabolic rate so you lose weight. But when you discontinue them, you gain the weight you've lost and usually some additional pounds as well. This often causes people to become depressed. Diet pills may also raise your blood pressure, or even trigger an arrhythmia.

I told Susan, "Diet pills are not the answer. Instead let's analyze your diet. What do you eat?"

She went through her typical day, which revolved around the usual sugar cycle. She'd crave sugar every three or four hours.

So I said, "Wait a second, Susan. Let's bring balance and restraint and temperance into your life. Let's just change a few eating habits. Let's cut out all sugars, all processed foods, all fried foods, and all junk foods. Instead you should start eating God's foods, living foods."

I recommended the right balance of lean proteins—not fried but grilled or baked or broiled. I also recommended good fats—fish oils, olive oils, avocados, macadamia nuts, and almonds.

Notice that I am not recommending a low-fat diet. That's not healthy. Our bodies have to have fat. We have over 60 trillion cells, and each cell has a fatty cell membrane. If we go on a low-fat diet, we may eventually become sick! Our cell membranes are not going to have what they need to repair themselves.

I also put Susan on healthy complex carbohydrates, such as brown rice, beans, and peas. I had her eat three good meals a day and two healthy snacks. And I recommended that she delegate different household chores to her two children. I even asked her husband to help her around the house with washing the dishes and vacuuming.

"Instead of drinking cappuccinos, sweet tea, and soft drinks, I want you to drink water with a lemon or lime or drink Pellegrino®" (sparkling water). I also suggested that she drink two quarts of water a day. "Let's watch what happens in the next few months as you do all this."

As a result of this regime Susan started sleeping eight hours a night and her energy returned. Now she was ready for a second step in her new approach to health. "I want you to get a buddy and start walking with her every other day or every day. Just walk about twenty minutes at a good clip, briskly enough so that you can't sing, but slow enough so that you can talk."

In six months Susan lost sixty pounds, ten pounds a month. She got off her diabetes and blood pressure medications, and her cholesterol returned to normal.

God has a plan for our lives: He wants us to walk in the Spirit so that we will not fulfill the lust of the flesh. The devil also has a plan: he wants us to keep lusting after the flesh. We must make a decision. God is not going to make this decision for us; He wants us to choose to restrain ourselves.

I often suggest that people begin with the following prayer of confession:

> *Father, forgive me for allowing my flesh to rule my Spirit man. I covenant this day to offer my body as a living sacrifice to You. I will no longer be controlled by the flesh. Instead I will walk in the Spirit. I declare today that I will practice temperance daily. I will restrain my flesh. I'll lay on Your altar my craving for sugar, chocolate, processed food, and ice cream. I'll do this for a season until You, Lord, give me permission to partake of them.*
>
> *Now, Lord, I confess divine health by faith. In the name of Jesus, high blood pressure has to leave. In the name of Jesus, high cholesterol has to leave. In the name of Jesus, all diseases must leave. I will walk in health because I am more than a conqueror. I can do all things through Christ who strengthens me. I vow to walk in love daily. I vow to walk in the Spirit. In Jesus' name. Amen.*

You will note that in this prayer I said "until You, Lord, give me permission to partake of them." People often ask me, "Will I always have to give up sugar?"

"Well, no," I say. "You can have a little on holidays—on Christmas and Thanksgiving and birthdays—as long as you do so in moderation. You can have one piece of cake or one piece of pie or a few cookies."

God expects us to treat our bodies as His temples. We've talked a lot in this chapter about what not to eat. At the end of Chapter Twelve, we will look at some of the foods Jesus ate to give us a Bible-based way of living and eating. I describe them in my book *What Would Jesus Eat?* These are the natural, God-made foods, and they lead to divine health.

Therefore if anyone cleanses himself from the latter, he will be a vessel for honor, sanctified and useful for the Master, prepared for every good work.
—2 TIMOTHY 2:21

chapter ten

The Favor of God:

A Lesson in Good Stewardship

"She considers a field and buys it; from her profits she plants a vineyard."
—PROVERBS 31:16

ow many of us think of money as the favor of God? Yet that's what it is. John told the first-century Christians, "Beloved, I pray that you may prosper in all things and be in health, just as your soul prospers" (3 John 1:2). Everything we have is God's gift to us, but a gift that also involves responsibility—and might even be used as a test for us.

In this chapter I'd like you to examine your attitude toward money from God's perspective in Scripture. I will ask you to answer four questions and compare your answers to Scriptures to determine your attitude toward money. Then you will use some worksheets to apply this knowledge to managing the money God has given you.

YOUR ATTITUDE TOWARD MONEY

Let's begin with a quick self-test. Check the statements below that apply to you:

_____ "Money helps me feel safe and secure."

_____ "I tend to believe that money is the source of happiness."

_____ "I worry about money and finances."

_____ "I sometimes tend to compromise my standards when it comes to money."

_____ "I know I should tithe to the church, but this is difficult for me."

Now let's look at the statements you checked.

1. "Money helps me feel safe and secure."

Solomon, one of the richest kings who ever lived, said this about money: "The rich think of their wealth as an impregnable defense; they imagine it is a high wall of safety" (Prov. 18:11 NLT).

How about you? Do you think that money can provide safety? Be honest now. One reason we all tend to want money is to live safely in a nice home with good food and material comforts. Again let me ask you to be truthful here. Do you think money will provide safety? If so, why?

_____

_____

Could you be wrong? _____ yes _____ no

If you are, how do you keep yourself from falling into this trap in the future? Write some ways to do so in the space below:

_____

_____

2. "I tend to believe that money is the source of happiness."

Many of us do believe that money will make us happy. If we just had a bigger house, nicer clothes, a bigger car, a vacation home. We might not think a crisp twenty dollar bill brings happiness, but many of us think that money provides the "stuff" that buys happiness. My husband often tells our congregation that we spend a lifetime collecting "things" and "things to put things on" and "things to pull behind things" and at the end of our lives the only "thing" they put in the box is us!

Paul wrote two letters to Timothy, the young pastor who became his protégé. As a youthful minister Timothy faced many challenges from the church and its surrounding culture. At the end of the first letter Paul warned Timothy about the prevailing attitudes about money.

> After all, we didn't bring anything with us when we came into the world, and we certainly cannot carry anything with us when we die. So if we have enough food and clothing, let us be content. But people who long to be rich fall into temptation and are trapped by many foolish and harmful desires that plunge them into ruin and destruction. For the love of money is at the root of all kinds of evil. And some people, craving money, have wandered from the faith and pierced themselves with many sorrows (1 Tim. 6:7–10 NLT).

Paul said "people who long to be rich fall into temptation and are trapped by many foolish and harmful desires that plunge them into ruin and destruction." Certainly this is true in our society. Counselors say that the two major reasons for divorce are adultery and finances.

Do you sometimes fall into temptation because you are trapped by foolish and harmful desires? If so, what are those desires? Write them in the space below.

_____

_____

_____

How can you overcome those desires? Write some thoughts in the space below:

_____

_____

Paul gives Timothy advice about how to overcome those harmful and foolish desires. This suggestion is also for you. Write your name in the blank space: "But you, _____, belong to God; so run from all these evil things, and follow what is right and good. Pursue a godly life, along with faith, love, perseverance, and gentleness" (1 Tim. 6:11 NLT).

Are you willing to "run from all these evil things"? A friend of mine stays far away from shopping centers and stores when she and her husband are short of funds. That's one way to run from evil. Can you think of others? Write them in the space below:

_____

_____

Take a minute now to consider what happens to people who love money. Remember, Paul warned Timothy, "For the love of money is at the root of all kinds of evil. And some people, craving money, have wandered from the faith and pierced themselves with many sorrows" (1 Tim. 6:10 NLT).

Have you been led astray? _____ yes _____ no
If you have, how have you done so? Note those ways in the space below:

_____

_____

Have you suffered self-inflicted sorrows? _____ yes _____ no

If you have, how have you done so? Be as honest as you can as you note those ways in the space below:

_____

_____

Obviously the early Christians tended to fall into the trap of loving money because Paul speaks again about this issue in his letter to the Hebrews. He says, "Stay away from the love of money; be satisfied with what you have" (Heb. 13:5 NLT).

Jesus also warned us: "Take heed and beware of covetousness, for one's life does not consist in the abundance of the things he possesses" (Luke 12:15).

As an antidote to loving money, Paul tells us to concentrate on a godly life, rather than on money and possessions. He says, "Pursue a godly life, along with faith, love, perseverance, and gentleness" (1 Tim. 6:11 NLT).

The same friend who avoids shopping centers when she has little money, also tries to align her life with God's perspective through prayer, daily Bible study, and faithful church attendance. This is an obvious answer; the key to the success of this strategy is a constant commitment to fulfill these goals.

What can you do to follow Paul's advice to pursue a godly life, along with faith, love, perseverance, and gentleness? Write those ideas in the space below:

_____

_____

_____

Finally Paul advised Timothy: "Tell those who are rich in this world not to be proud and not to trust in their money, which will soon be gone. But their trust should be in the living God, who richly gives us all we need for our enjoyment" (1 Tim. 6:17 NLT).

3. "I worry about money and finances."

Most people would check this statement. No matter how rich, many of us worry about our finances. In fact, those who have more often spend way beyond what they should, and therefore tend to worry even more.

Jesus addressed this problem in the Sermon on the Mount. Many of us are familiar with what He said. "No one can serve two masters; for either he will hate the one and love the other, or else he will be loyal to the one and despise the other. You cannot serve God and mammon. Therefore I say to you, do not worry about your life, what you will eat or what you will drink; nor about your body, what you will put on. Is not life more than food and the body more than clothing?" (Matt. 6:24–25).

He repeated this warning before He ended His thoughts about our tendency to worry. "Therefore do not worry about tomorrow, for tomorrow will worry about its own things. Sufficient for the day is its own trouble" (Matt. 6:34).

Most of us are familiar with these passages. The trick comes in actually being able to live by what Jesus said when the bills mount up or the refrigerator breaks down and the car needs expensive repairs. What do we naturally do? We worry.

And this kind of worry is actually fear. Fear that we won't have enough to support our family. Fear that we might lose our jobs and eventually lose our homes. Fear of what might happen in the future.

But what do we really accomplish when we worry?

Counselors note that their patients suffer when they worry. They . . .

- Damage their health
- Disrupt their productivity
- Reduce their ability to trust in God.

Often worry means that our possessions are becoming too important to us. This means we might have to do some cutting back or simplifying.

Think about your life. Are your possessions becoming too important to you? How might you change this? Mention some ways in the space below:

_____

_____

Jesus ends His discussion of money with a promise: "But seek first the kingdom of God and His righteousness, and all these things shall be added to you" (Matt. 6:33).

Trust me, Jesus says. I will supply your needs. The Lord is asking you to trust Him for He has promised to supply all of your needs.

4. "I sometimes tend to compromise my standards when it comes to money."

Jesus told a parable about a shrewd manager whose employer heard that the man was being dishonest. The rich employer told the man he was to get his accounts in order because he was going to be fired so the man devised a devious plan. He called those who owed his employer and reduced their debts. That way, the manager thought he was making friends for the future when he would be out of work. These people would owe him a favor. And you can be sure he would ask them to ante up.

Christ ended this parable with the following warning:

"Unless you are faithful in small matters, you won't be faithful in large ones. If you cheat even a little, you won't be honest with greater responsibilities. And if you are untrustworthy about worldly wealth, who will trust you with the true riches of heaven? And if you are not faithful with other people's money, why should you be trusted with money of your own? No one can serve two masters. For you will hate one and love the other, or be devoted to one and despise the other. You cannot serve both God and money" (Luke 16:10–13 NLT).

What does your attitude toward money say about your character? Have you been honest in small matters, such as your expense account or your income tax return? Think about your own life and note the ways you might have compromised your integrity:

_____

_____

Now think about Jesus' warning: "Unless you are faithful in small matters, you won't be faithful in large ones. If you cheat even a little, you won't be honest with greater responsibilities. And if you are untrustworthy about worldly wealth who will trust you with the true riches of heaven?"

Think about those words the next time you are tempted to fudge just a little on your expense account or adjust your time card to meet your hourly quota.

5. "I know I should tithe to the church, but this is difficult for me."

In Malachi 3, God accuses His people of robbing Him. Then He asks a rhetorical question: "But you say, in what way have we robbed You?" The response? "In tithes and offerings. You are cursed with a curse for you have robbed Me" (vv. 8–9).

We live in financial bondage if we do not honor God with our tithes and offerings. Jesus said, "Give and it will be given to you: good measure, pressed down, shaken together, and running over. . . . For with the same measure that you use, it will be measured back to you" (Luke 6:38).

When we release what's in our hands toward God, He releases what's in His hand toward us. Personally I prefer His blessings to my "things."

Unfortunately some people do not realize this. My husband teaches that there are two kinds of givers: the reason giver and the revelation giver. Reason givers are driven by carnal objections that say, "My resources are limited so I can give very little because I have little." Revelation givers see God as their financial source and give to God, based on God's ability to give to them.

Fortunately John and I have seen reason givers become revelation givers. One example is directly from the Bible. The prophet Elijah walked into a widow's house and basically said, "I want to eat the last piece of bread you've got."

The widow answered, "I don't have any bread, only a little flour and some oil. Haven't you heard," she said, "we've got a real drought and famine in our land?" This widow was a reason giver. If she had continued to think that way, she might have thrown the preacher out of her house and saved that flour for herself and her son.

Instead she believed Elijah when he repeated God's promise: "For thus says the LORD God of Israel: 'The bin of flour shall not be used up, nor shall the jar of oil run dry, until the day the LORD sends rain on the earth'" (1 Kings 17:14).

Now the widow saw God as her source of infinite supply, so she used her last bit of flour to make bread for Elijah. At the moment she gave this to the prophet her barrel of oil was filled. This widow had an unlimited supply for the balance of the drought because she gave to the man of God for the purposes of God.

As a pastor's wife and a believing Christian I have always tithed. Several years ago I was reading about the firstfruits and how the Lord demanded that the Israelites give their firstfruits to Him. I always gave God His tithe within the calendar year, but often it would not be the first check I wrote out of my checkbook. If there was a child's college tuition payment or a special insurance payment or an unexpected debt, I would often pay that first. Then if I didn't have enough for our tithe that week, I would make it up with the next week's paycheck. Once I realized the importance of firstfruits, I repented and asked the Lord to forgive me. From that day forward the first check I wrote was our tithe.

Do you tithe to your church? If not, please read Malachi 3:10. You are to bring your tithe to the storehouse, which represents God's house or your church where you receive spiritual food. God provides 100 percent of our income and only asks us to give one tenth back to Him in order for us to receive His blessings.

Are you willing to give God His due? _____ yes _____ no

Now that you've analyzed your attitude toward money, let's look at how you are currently spending what God has given you. Ron Blue, a financial advisor and founder of Ronald Blue & Company, a professional investment firm, says "My role as a financial advisor is to help you discover what God would have you learn, either from your financial abundance or apparent lack of financial resources. God is not trying to frustrate you; God is trying to get your attention—and money is a great attention-getter.

"Money is not only a tool, but also a test in managing someone else's resources. If your checkbook precedes you to Heaven could you confidently expect God to say as you stood before Him, 'Well done, good and faithful servant'? Is that hope unrealistic? Not at all. It is God's desire and intention—He wants it more than you do."[1]

Walk through the following two worksheets with me so you can analyze how you are spending your money.

The first worksheet is an analysis of your living expenses; the second worksheet is a cash flow analysis.

LIVING EXPENSES

	Amount Paid Monthly	Amount Paid Other Than Monthly	Total Annual
FIRST FRUITS			
Tithe	_____	_____	_____
(10% of gross income)			
Offering	_____	_____	_____
Total	_____	_____	_____
HOUSING			
Mortgage/rent	_____	_____	_____
Insurance	_____	_____	_____
Property taxes	_____	_____	_____
Electricity	_____	_____	_____
Heating	_____	_____	_____
Garbage pickup	_____	_____	_____
Telephone	_____	_____	_____
Repairs/maintenance	_____	_____	_____
Other	_____	_____	_____
Total Housing	_____	_____	_____
FOOD	_____	_____	_____

	Amount Paid Monthly	Amount Paid Other Than Monthly	Total Annual
CLOTHING			
Husband			
Wife			
Children			
Total Clothing			
TRANSPORTATION			
Car payment			
Insurance			
Gas			
Repair/maintenance			
Other			
Total Transportation			
ENTERTAINMENT			
Eating out			
Babysitters			
Magazines/newspapers			
Cable TV			
Vacation			
Clubs/activities			
Classes/courses			

	Amount Paid Monthly	Amount Paid Other Than Monthly	Total Annual
Other	_____	_____	_____
Total Entertainment	_____	_____	_____
MEDICAL EXPENSES			
Insurance	_____	_____	_____
Doctor	_____	_____	_____
Dentist	_____	_____	_____
Prescriptions	_____	_____	_____
Total Medical Expenses	_____	_____	_____
INSURANCE	_____	_____	_____
Life	_____	_____	_____
Disability	_____	_____	_____
Other	_____	_____	_____
Total Insurance	_____	_____	_____
CHILDREN			
Child Support	_____	_____	_____
School lunches	_____	_____	_____
Allowances	_____	_____	_____
Tuition	_____	_____	_____

	Amount Paid Monthly	Amount Paid Other Than Monthly	Total Annual
Lessons (tutoring, music, etc.)	_____	_____	_____
Sports	_____	_____	_____
Other	_____	_____	_____
Total Children	_____	_____	_____
GIFTS			
Christmas	_____	_____	_____
Birthdays	_____	_____	_____
Anniversary	_____	_____	_____
Other	_____	_____	_____
Total Gifts	_____	_____	_____
MISCELLANEOUS			
Toiletries	_____	_____	_____
Dry cleaning	_____	_____	_____
Animal care	_____	_____	_____
Beauty/barber	_____	_____	_____
Other	_____	_____	_____
Total Miscellaneous	_____	_____	_____

	Amount Paid Monthly	Amount Paid Other Than Monthly	Total Annual
WORK RELATED EXPENSES			
Lunches			
Parking			
Mass transit or commute			
Union dues			
Other			
Total Work Expenses			
ADDITIONAL DEBT			
Credit cards			
Personal loans			
Other			
Total Additional Debt			
TOTAL LIVING EXPENSES			
Housing			
Food			
Clothing			
Transportation			
Entertainment			
Medical			
Insurance			

	Amount Paid Monthly	Amount Paid Other Than Monthly	Total Annual
Children	_____	_____	_____
Gifts	_____	_____	_____
Miscellaneous	_____	_____	_____
Work related	_____	_____	_____
Additional debt	_____	_____	_____
Total Living Expenses	_____	_____	_____

Now look at your cash flow by filling in the analysis below.

CASH FLOW ANALYSIS

	Monthly	Annual
Net Income on paycheck Husband	_____	_____
Wife	_____	_____
Other (child support, etc.)	_____	_____
Total Income	_____	_____
Total Living Expenses	_____	_____
Spendable Income	_____	_____

Once you have completed these two worksheets, you will have some idea of where you stand financially. If you desire a more complete analysis, you might want to look at Ron Blue's *Master Your Money Workbook*.

Finally, remember God's principles of financial prosperity:

Principle One: He who will not work, will not eat (1 Tim. 5:8).

Application: Get a job and maintain a godly witness in your employment.

Principle Two: Bring all the tithes into the storehouse (Mal. 3:10).

Application: Tithe to your church.

Principle Three: Neither a borrower nor a lender be (Prov. 22:7).

Application: Stop spending outside your budget.

Principle Four: Give and it will be given unto you (2 Cor. 9:10–11).

Application: Give your tithe and offering and expect an increase.

The Word of God tells us not to worry about what we should wear or what we should eat, but to trust in Him. He will meet all of our needs.

Make me walk along the path of your commands, for that is where my happiness is found. Give me an eagerness for your decrees; do not inflict me with love for money! Turn my eyes from worthless things, and give me life through your word.

—PSALM 119:35–37 NLT

chapter eleven

Hospitality:

An Attitude of the Heart

Be hospitable to one another without grumbling."

—I Peter 4:9

Someone once asked Perle Mesta, the great Washington hostess, the secret of her success in getting so many rich and famous people to attend her parties. "It's all in the goodbyes," she said. She went on to explain that as each guest arrived, she met him or her with "At last you're here," and as each one of them left, she expressed her regrets with "I'm so sorry you have to leave so soon."

Pearl realized our intrinsic need to be accepted and appreciated because down deep most of us feel somewhat disconnected from those around us. I am amazed by the loneliness in the world today.

I recently received a letter from a new Jewish friend who was a guest at our "Night To Honor Israel" program at Cornerstone Church. Let me share a portion of that letter with you:

I want to express, once again, my deepest gratitude and appreciation for all the arrangements you made for me, for your special invitation, and for your great kindness and hospitality. In Judaism, we have a religious obligation known as *Hachnasat Orchim*. This is often translated as "hospitality." We first learn about *Hachnasat Orchim* in the Book of Genesis, at the moment when Abraham and Sarah were visited by angels who came to share the news with them that Sarah would conceive a child. The hospitality that you have demonstrated to me is of this highest order, and I will forever be thankful.

I was very humbled by this woman's kind words. I wanted to know more about *Hachnasat Orchim* so I called our dear friend Rabbi Scheinberg and asked him to provide more information about this biblical obligation. He sent me *The Jewish Religion: A Companion,* which gave a definition of hospitality:

> *Hachnasat Ochim* is translated from Hebrew as "bringing in guests." In Judaism this is considered to be a *mitzvah,* a high religious obligation. The prototype is the patriarch Abraham who sits at the door of his tent ready to welcome hungry and thirsty travelers, Genesis 18:18. Since the narrative states that the Lord appeared to Abraham and yet Abraham ran to welcome his guests, a Rabbinic comment has that to welcome the Devine Presence, the *Shekhinah.* Another Rabbinic comment is that Abraham's tent had an opening on all four sides so that he could run to welcome guests from whichever direction they came. In Eastern Europe a house in which generous hospitality is provided was known as "a house with Abraham, our father's doors." [1]

Note that even though Abraham was in God's presence, he left the Lord and ran to welcome his guests. That's how important hospitality is. I believe to welcome a guest into your home with hospitality is to welcome the presence of the Holy One, the Shekinah Glory of the Living God.

There's nothing like receiving someone in your home for a meal, since a meal is the bread that God has so richly and abundantly provided for His people. As I said in *The King's Daughter* hospitality is now a lost art, and we need to preserve it before it becomes extinct.

One of the best-known stories about hospitality in the Bible is the story of Martha's entertaining Jesus. Martha bustles around, while her sister Mary sits quietly at the feet of Jesus. Most of us can associate with Martha. We've been there. We've had so much to do, and so little time to do it, that we've exploded in frustration. Usually our families receive these outbursts. Martha took this one step further: She let Jesus know that Mary was not carrying her full share of the burden of hospitality that day. To put it bluntly, she whined. "Lord," Martha said, "do You not care that my sister has left me to serve alone? Therefore tell her to help me" (Luke 10:40).

J. Vernon McGee understands Martha's dilemma. He says, "Martha was a dear soul and if it had not been for her they would not have had that lovely dinner. She got busy, however, and became frustrated. Possibly she reached for a pan, thought it was not big enough, then reached for another, and a pan fell off the top shelf. It was too much for her and she came walking out of the kitchen, and said something which she would not have said under normal conditions."[2]

What did Jesus reply to Martha's request that Mary help her? He didn't instruct Mary to do so. No, instead He said, "Martha, Martha, you are worried and troubled about many things. But one thing is needed, and Mary has chosen that good part, which will not be taken away from her" (Luke 10:41–42). Jesus clearly said: I will not tell Mary to rush into the kitchen; instead you need to join her and listen to what I am saying.

Now it's easy for us to criticize Martha. We can think, "Her concentration on small details might have made people uncomfortable. The personal attention she gave her guests should be more important," we reason, "than the comforts she tried to provide for them."

Yet even though my intentions were pure, I have found myself aggravated by small things that are not going exactly right for a dinner party. Through the years I have learned that it is not perfection, or even the food guests are hungering for, it is the love and the joyful spirit in which I receive them.

Now, when I prepare my functions I call on the name of the Lord: *Lord, I am having friends for dinner tonight. I need Your help. Allow my attitude to be right before You. I want my guests to feel Your presence as they walk through the door. Accept this meal as a loving sacrifice of praise unto Your throne. Amen.*

Recently, I had a wedding reception in our home for a young lady who is my namesake. I have known her family for over thirty years, and I was excited to present a perfect celebration for this deserving young lady. We were expecting over two hundred people and I had beautiful plans for our back yard to receive all our guests.

Well, wouldn't you know, even though the day before was an absolutely gorgeous fall day, the day of the wedding brought a downpour. Years ago I would have panicked, but for what? I was determined to have a fabulous celebration of a beautiful sacrament so I prayed, *Lord, Your Word states that rain is a blessing from You for it gives us the ability to grow the food You so abundantly provide. I receive this blessing and I ask You to help me make this day a memorable one for our bride. Allow our guests to feel Your presence as they walk through the door and make them feel they have been received by Your Spirit. Amen.*

Right after this, my husband came into the kitchen and asked, "What are you going to do?"

"*We* are going to move furniture and bring all the decorations into the house," I answered. Thankfully a group of wonderful friends soon came through my doors, and they also began to help me prepare my home for this grand occasion. I knew God had heard my prayer when I heard laughter fill our home, even though the rain was pouring down as we were scurrying to move all those chairs and tables.

Once the guests arrived, I was astonished at the Lord's provision. Remember, we were expecting over two hundred people. I could almost feel my home expand as it received person after person after person. Smiles and laughter continued to dominate the atmosphere. The bride and groom were radiant, I was thrilled, and I knew God was pleased.

Take a moment now to think about the last time you entertained guests. Describe that experience in the space below:

_____

_____

_____

_____

Now analyze the situation. Check the statements below that accurately reflect this experience:

_____ You prepared ahead of time so that you weren't sweeping the kitchen floor as your guests arrived (or preparing the salad or setting the table).

_____ You were calm and collected and didn't scream at your family to help you or snap at them because you were running so late.

_____ You greeted your friends at the door, looking rested and pleased that they were your guests.

_____ You sat and talked to your friends before and after the meal.

_____ You spent more time with your friends than you did in the kitchen.

If you were able to check all of these statements, give yourself a healthy pat on the back. If you were only able to check two, take a moment now to think about how you could change your habits in the future so that you could be a pleasant balance between Mary and Martha. List some ways in the space on the next page:

_____

_____

_____

All of us have some *measure* of hospitality within us. When we accept Jesus Christ as our Lord and Savior and ask Him to come into our hearts, He does exactly that: He moves in. Jesus Christ is love. Therefore, we can't help but show His love to others as we receive people into our homes.

Yet some of us actually have the *gift* of hospitality. You have this gift if you have no trouble receiving few or many into your home, and you look for ways to entertain your friends and family. You actually derive joy from the experience!

Don't feel discouraged if you can't entertain twenty-five people at a time. Whether you are serving dinner to your husband and children or to your extended family the Lord requires the spirit of hospitality to be in your heart and on your lips.

Karen Mains, who was a pastor's wife of an inner city church that met in a rented facility, wrote one of the first books on Christian hospitality, *Open Heart, Open Home*. In this book, she told of how she responded with pride, rather than hospitality, when two friends stopped by, unannounced, right after she and David were married.

Later, when she told her mother about their visit, her mother replied, "You mean you spent the evening on the front porch and didn't invite them inside! Karen! Haven't you heard your father insist I must never put my pride before my hospitality?" [3]

True hospitality comes before pride, Karen maintains. And this was a lesson that was hard-won for her. "Because so many of our church activities are conducted in our homes, for many years it seemed as though I did nothing but clean up after people. One group would leave. I would vacuum. Another group would come and go. I would straighten. Another would eat. I would wash dishes." [4]

How did Karen turn this around?

First she realized the difference between secular entertaining and Christian hospitality. "Entertaining always puts things before people. 'As soon as I get the house finished, the living room decorated, my place settings complete, my housecleaning done—then I will start having people in.' 'The So-and-so's are coming. I must buy that new such-and-such before they come.' Hospitality, however, puts people before things. 'We have no furniture; we'll eat on the floor.'

"Entertaining says, 'I want to impress you with my beautiful home, my clever decorating, my gourmet cooking.' Hospitality, however, seeks to minister. It says, 'This home is not mine. It is truly a gift from my Master. I am His servant and I use it as He desires.' Hospitality does not try to impress, but to serve.[5]

I've begun this chapter with entertaining others, since Scripture tells us to open our homes for fellowship. The author of Hebrews told the Jewish believers: "Don't forget to show hospitality to strangers, for some who have done this have entertained angels without realizing it!" (13:2 NLT). And the apostle Paul told the Romans, "When God's children are in need, be the one to help them out. And get into the habit of inviting guests home for dinner or, if they need lodging, for the night" (Rom. 12:13 NLT).

But we don't want to forget to entertain our own family by dining together at home.

DINING TOGETHER AT HOME

Unfortunately some families do not eat together. David Lowenstein, a psychologist and family counselor, noted, "Studies have found that 70% of American families don't eat meals together every week. Those who do are likely to have family dinners once or twice a week."[6]

In their book, *The Gift of Cooking with Joy*, Joy Stuart, Kim Bucey, and Sherri Carswell give seven reasons for dining together at home:

- The family benefits by learning to value one another.
- Children receive stability, especially in times of crisis.
- Children may succeed better in school.
- The family enjoys laughter and fun together.
- The family benefits by sharing sacred moments.
- The family establishes sacred traditions.
- The family is blessed by praying together.[7]

Each of these reasons is supported by factual information that confirms these benefits. I'd like to look at one of those now: The family benefits by dining together at home.

Hospitality, I believe, begins at home. The rule at our house when our children lived with us was that we eat the evening meal together. During our meal we discussed the events of the day, trying to concentrate on the children as much as possible. We struggled to keep the laughter that dominates any topic to a low roar. Usually the more serious I tried to be, the more the children considered it a challenge to make laughter the goal.

I know they will remember the dinner long after they forget what I served, because the joy and security that comes from that special time together will never be forgotten. I always felt honored when they asked, as they often did, to invite a friend over for dinner.

Much to my dismay I've found that having dinner at home around the table in America has become an endangered species. I know that many of you are working mothers who are often overwhelmed by your busy schedules. I know how it is—I've been there. I've been blessed by having a very understanding husband and terrific kids who are willing to adjust to hectic schedules.

My first rule is this: Don't allow yourself to feel overwhelmed! The meal will get done if you plan properly. When you have a light day, plan to make several main dishes for future meals. These can be anything from casseroles to spaghetti sauce to chili and taco meat.

Store these in your freezer and plan the week's menu around them. You'll find that selecting a previously prepared main dish from your freezer in the morning, then adding a salad, bread, and a vegetable to the meal that night will make your evenings at home a lot less stressful.

Another helpful hint is to set the table before you leave for work in the morning. Doing this task in advance will allow you to put your feet up for awhile before you serve dinner. The less stress you experience, the more the dinner hour will be a pleasant experience for you and your family.

You might say to me, "Diana, I hate to cook!" But you don't have to enjoy cooking to put together a really great meal for yourself or your family. Always remember that you are doing more than sustaining life with food: You are creating an atmosphere of love and security in an otherwise stressful environment.

Think about your own family. How can you be sure your family will eat together at home? List those ways in the space below:

_____

_____

_____

Before I close this chapter, let me challenge you to look at your own church and your own neighborhood to see if there are some ways you can use your gift of hospitality.

SHARING THE GIFT OF HOSPITALITY

In her book, Karen Mains suggests that each of us take a moment to consider our own churches and neighborhoods. Answer these three questions:

1. Are the homes of the members of your church open or closed to one another? _____ yes _____ no

2. Are the homes in your neighborhood open or closed to one another? _____ yes _____ no

3. How would you rate the climate of community in your congregation?

_____ excellent. We are a true community of believers.

_____ good. We have dinner groups, Wednesday evening fellowships, and other activities that encourage us to spend time together.

_____ fair. I sometimes spend time with members of the church outside of formal services.

_____ poor. I go to service but really don't know anyone in the church.

If you checked excellent or good, you are experiencing the type of community found in the New Testament church. If you checked fair or poor, what do you think you could do to improve the climate in your church? List some ideas in the space below:

_____

_____

_____

Now think about your neighborhood. How would you rate the climate there?

_____ excellent. We frequently spend time together. We have neighborhood block parties and other activities.

_____ good. We care for one another every so often. If someone is sick, we prepare food for them.

_____ fair. If I really need help, I could probably ask a neighbor for help.

_____ poor. I never really see my neighbors. We are all too busy.

If you checked excellent or good, you are living in a great neighborhood. If you checked fair or poor, what could you do to create a better feeling of community within your neighborhood? List some ideas in the space below:

_____

_____

_____

Remember, outside your family, your neighborhood is the greatest opportunity to witness to others about Jesus Christ. Paul tells us in the book of Philemon: "I pray that you may be active in sharing your faith, so that you will have a full understanding of every good thing we have in Christ" (1:6 NIV).

One woman I know was willing to use her gift of hospitality to help others. In 1997, Joy Stuart was attending a relaxing ladies luncheon and cooking seminar on food and Southern culture. When culinary artist Nathalie Dupree began cooking on stage, Joy became fascinated by the attitudes and comments of the women at her table who quickly lamented the numerous reasons why they did not cook much anymore. She could hear several of the women say, "My family just doesn't eat together very often anymore."

As Joy sat in that hotel ballroom she heard God speaking to her heart. He reminded her of the many joys their family had experienced while eating dinner together. Soon a vision began to unfold of how she might encourage women of all ages from various backgrounds to learn a way of cooking, based on the biblical principles of cooking with the divine joy of the Lord.

Joy shared this vision with Mary Ann Ruff, the director of women's ministry at her church. "I would like to teach Cooking with Joy classes as part of the women's ministry discipleship and outreach program for women." Mary Ann agreed that this vision reflected the heartbeat of the women's ministry at the church: "to love God and love your neighbor."

These cooking classes would also be an easy way for newcomers who were not familiar with the Bible to become part of the small group program in the church. Some of these women would then be open to joining a small Bible study group.

From 1998 through 2002, Joy Stuart enlisted help from Kimberly Bucey, a knowledgeable cook, and Sherri Carswell, a home economist. These three women found that many women today do not cook in their kitchens because no one ever taught them how to cook.

Finally Joy, Kimberly, and Sherri published their book, *The Gift of Cooking with Joy*, which includes thirteen chapters of practical cooking advice, based on biblical principles, such as equipping your kitchen, basic nutrition, and meal planning; twelve cooking lessons to start this ministry in your church or neighborhood; and 120 recipes, 24 of which were actually cooked in the Cooking with Joy classes.[8]

Because Joy Stuart was willing to heed the Lord's direction, she has seen God move in the hearts of women in her church. Could the Lord be calling you to use your gift of hospitality in your own church or neighborhood?

For you, brethren, have been called to liberty; only do not use liberty as an opportunity for the flesh, but through love serve one another. For all the law is fulfilled in one word, even in this: "You shall love your neighbor as yourself."

—GALATIANS 5:13–14

chapter twelve

Beauty:

A Mirrored Reflection of Christ

*"Let your light so shine before men, that they may see your good works
and glorify your Father in heaven.*

—MATTHEW 5:16

When my doctor was reviewing the results of my tests after a well check, he said, "You need to lose 15 percent of your body weight." That didn't sound too alarming to me so I nodded graciously, thanked him for his suggestions, and left his office.

The next morning as I was taking a shower I calculated what 15 percent of my body weight would be, by writing the equation on the fogged-up glass door. Once the calculation was finished I got angry. How could I lose that much? I didn't really think I needed to.

I admit that I'm a large woman. I'm tall, 5 feet, 7 inches. I'm wide in the shoulders and the hips. I've got long legs and arms. But I think I carry my weight well. I thought, *I should have slapped the man!*

Unfortunately many of us equate beauty with our physical appearance. I believe there's so much more to being beautiful, and that's what I'd like us to explore in this chapter.

THE BIBLICAL CONCEPT OF BEAUTY

Esther was a young woman who "was lovely and beautiful" (Esther 2:7). Her beauty, grace, and character shone, bright and unwavering, against the darkness threatening the Jewish people. Esther even had a beauty regimen that was mentioned in the Bible, which motivated the Woman of God seminars.

God created each one of us with beautiful and unique characteristics. It is not difficult to establish a personal regimen that is individualized to our unique traits. Yet once many women marry, they feel it is no longer necessary to maintain their outer appearance; they assume that their husbands are not going anywhere. Sad to report, this is not the case. We often fall into the adversary's trap and lose much more than our outer beauty when we stop caring about our appearance.

After twenty years of marriage or a single lifestyle, some of us are overwhelmed by the idea of a makeover of our image, but it takes only desire, time, and dedication to become the woman God intended for each of us to be. Let's look now at the three makeover steps I suggested to the women who attended the Woman of God seminars.

THREE MAKEOVER STEPS

The first step in your Woman of God makeover is to pray.

STEP ONE: PRAY

Some people have given the inscription ASAP a new meaning. They suggest that the initials signify: Always Say A Prayer. I second their interpretation. The first step is always to pray.

Stop now to ask God to reveal how He sees you. Often what you consider ugly, He sees as beautiful. Write a prayer on the next page, asking Him to show you your beautiful and unique characteristics:

———————————————————————————

———————————————————————————

———————————————————————————

Now note those characteristics, both outward and inward, that are revealed to you as you take a moment to meditate on God's answer.

———————————————————————————

———————————————————————————

———————————————————————————

Our inner appearance should match our outward appearance if we are to be true daughters of the King. Jesus warned the Pharisees: "Woe to you, scribes and Pharisees, hypocrites! For you are like whitewashed tombs which indeed appear beautiful outwardly, but inside are full of dead men's bones and all uncleanness. Even so you also outwardly appear righteous to men, but inside you are full of hypocrisy and lawlessness" (Matt. 23:27–28).

I've asked you to focus on what is beautiful in a woman, now let me tell you what God sees as ugly. The apostle Peter warned the early Christians, "Do not let your adornment be merely outward—arranging the hair, wearing gold, or putting on fine apparel—rather let it be the hidden person of the heart, with the incorruptible beauty of a gentle and quiet spirit, which is very precious in the sight of God" (1 Peter 3:3–4).

The second step to take in your makeover is to make sure you are spiritually in balance.

STEP TWO: CHECK YOUR SPIRITUAL BALANCE

I have seen women who were striking outwardly, yet perceived themselves as ugly because their spiritual life was out of God's will.

How about you? Certain practices lead to spiritual balance. Check the practices below that you are currently practicing:

_____ "I practice some solitude. I spend time alone with the Father."

_____ "I study and meditate on Scripture to keep my focus on God's ways."

_____ "I spend time in prayer each day."

_____ "I worship God both with other Christians and when I am alone."

_____ "I spend time with other Christians. I am accountable to another Christian."

If you were unable to check many of these statements, ask God what you must do to get back in fellowship with Him and His people. Scripture promises "that He who has begun a good work in you will complete it until the day of Jesus Christ" (Phil. 1:6).

Write a prayer in the space below, asking the Lord to help you become more balanced in your spiritual walk.

_____

_____

_____

The final step is to make a list of the things that need to be done to enhance your personal appearance.

STEP THREE: ENHANCE YOUR APPEARANCE

Scripture tells us that our bodies are sacred. "Do you not know that your body is the temple of the Holy Spirit who is in you, whom you have from God, and you are not your own?" (1 Cor. 6:19). God expects us to pay attention to our physical health.

Your physical health

If you are over eighteen, it is essential that you go to the gynecologist for an annual exam. If you are over forty, you should have a mammogram once a year or as prescribed by your doctor. If you are beyond menopause, you should have a yearly physical by a family practitioner or internist. And every five years you should have a colonoscopy. You also should have a dental checkup and a cleaning at least twice a year.

How about you? Fill in the blanks below:

The last time I had an annual exam was _____.
Therefore I should schedule an appointment for (mention the particular month):
_____.
The last time I had a dental checkup was _____.
Therefore I should schedule an appointment for _____.

Your posture

Do you always stand up straight? Unfortunately some women tend to slump and round their shoulders. That's quite easy to do, especially as we get older. Some bras are made to help correct poor posture. My friend who has one of these bras says she hates to wear it because of the pull on her shoulders, but she knows that it helps her to stand straighter when she is wearing it and to remember to do so when she isn't.

Your hair

How about your hair? Do you get it cut regularly? _____ yes _____ no
Some of us feel insecure here. We wonder, *What do I do? Where do I go?* Take a deep breath and ask yourself, *Do I know someone who always looks great?* Call her and ask where she goes to have her hair done.

Another obstacle is expense. Most hair salons that employ professional stylists charge higher prices than many women can afford. I tell my Woman of God class to start a beauty jar, which can hold any extra change they may have after groceries are bought or even loose change in their purses. "Before long you will be surprised by how much you have accumulated," I say, "maybe enough for a professional haircut every six to eight weeks." If you have a good haircut, you can easily manage your hair between visits.

Unfortunately many women who are stay-at-home moms think that the family's money should be spent on their husbands' and children's clothes. After all, they are out in the business world and at school all day.

Not so. These women have just as much right to spend money on their hair and their clothes. However, remember the word *moderation*. Don't try to do in one week what you haven't done in years.

Your clothes

How long has it been since you have purchased new clothes for yourself? Dressing well is not always as expensive as we might think. Susan Wales in her book, *The Art of Romantic Living*, tells the story of Lillie Langtry, who was dubbed the "maven of elegance" by Victorian England. Lillie could not afford a costly gown, like the ones worn at this time, so she arrived at a London social event in a plain black dress. Among the ornate gowns, Lillie stood out.

The next morning the society pages were full of glowing descriptions of Lillie, and numerous social invitations began to arrive. That night Lillie lowered the neckline and twisted her hair into a knot. The following evening she added a cloche hat, and the night after that she added feathers to the dress. Each night she accessorized or altered the dress, and no one seemed to realize that this was the same black dress.[1]

Soon the dress shops in London copied Lillie's classic black dress, a trend that even crossed the Atlantic to America. No one captivated the city of London like this naïve vicar's daughter from Jersey.

Accessorizing, Susan Wales says, is the secret of romantic fashion. She gives several suggestions as to how you can vary a basic black dress:

- Fling a fringed shawl over your shoulders. A large scarf, she says, can also double as a shawl.
- Add a jacket or coat.
- Wear a long or three-quarter-length sweater, either open or buttoned.
- Add a faux-fur vest or a faux-fur or lace collar.
- Tie a sweater around your shoulders. Place one sleeve on top of the other and then turn up the ends and cuff together.[2]

Susan Wales suggests that the basic black dress should be a mainstay to any woman's clothes closet. Stop now to take an inventory of your wardrobe. Start with the present season. Then when the season changes, go through this process again. Write the clothes you have in the space below:

Slacks and blue jeans

_____

_____

_____

Susan Wales suggests that jeans can be dressed up—by adding a necklace, earrings, and bracelets or a blazer—or down by wearing them with a t-shirt.

Dresses

_____

_____

_____

Susan suggests a printed silk or synthetic dress in your favorite design and color as a possible second dress.

Blazer or suits

_____

_____

_____

Susan suggests a navy-blue blazer that can be worn with blue jeans or Kahki and white pants. She also suggests trousers in solid colors of black, navy, khaki, gray, and white, which can be worn with a jacket as a pants suit.

Skirts

_____

_____

_____

Again Susan suggests simple classics to begin a wardrobe. A denim skirt, a khaki skirt, and a flowing peasant skirt in white. The style can be long or short and straight or pleated.

Shoes

_____

_____

_____

Choose classic dress shoes in bone and black, Susan says, because they go with most outfits.[3] Obviously everyone needs a couple pairs of casual shoes, like tennis shoes and thongs.

Now what do you need to add to your wardrobe? Mention those items in the space below:

Slacks and blue jeans

_____

_____

Dresses

_____

_____

Blazer or suits

_____

_____

Skirts

_____

_____

Shoes

_____

_____

If you are interested in updating your wardrobe, know that some of the major discount family stores are carrying great clothing styles at very reasonable prices.

Fortunately there are discount malls in most cities where you can purchase name-brand clothes for less. And many women buy their clothes at the end of the season for the next year. That's when stores have inventory-reduction sales.

There are also "next-to-new" and consignment shops in most cities today. Often you can get designer clothes at low prices. One of my friends looked absolutely stunning at her son's wedding. Several weeks after the wedding I commented on her beautiful dress and asked where she got it (thinking I might like to shop there myself).

"Do you promise not to tell anyone?"

I agreed, but now I'm writing about this in a book, but I'm not giving her name.

"I got this dress from a resale shop. After the wedding I sold it on consignment and got more for the dress than I paid for it. I knew I would never wear that elaborate a dress again."

All of us need to realize that we don't need to buy our clothes at the most expensive shop in town to look good. Susan Wales's book, *The Art of Romantic Living*, also gives further ideas for creating an inexpensive, stylish wardrobe.

THE TEMPLE OF THE LORD

The apostle Paul referred to our bodies as temples of the Holy Spirit: "Or do you not know that your body is the temple of the Holy Spirit who is in you, whom you have from God, and you are not your own? For you were bought at a price; therefore glorify God in your body and in your spirit, which are God's" (1 Cor. 6:19–20).

References to good health are found throughout Scripture. The Lord gave the Israelites dietary laws to preserve their health (Lev. 11), and science has now confirmed that those laws are linked to preventive medicine and long life. James encouraged those who were sick to go to the elders of the church and request anointing with oil and prayer (James 5:14). Solomon stated that the wisdom of the Lord was "health to your flesh, and strength to your bones" (Prov. 3:8). What kind of wisdom are we using to maintain our bodies?

Dr. Don Colbert has written the book *What Would Jesus Eat?* in which he calls Christians to adopt Jesus' example. At the end of each chapter, Colbert has a boxed-in statement that answers the question, "What would Jesus eat?" We can use six of these statements to plan our own menus.

1. Jesus ate whole grains directly and in the form of whole-grain bread.

We can follow His example, Colbert says, by choosing to eat whole-grain breads and pastas and to eat whole grains in cooked and salad dishes.[4]

Think about your meal plans for the next two weeks. What can you include to increase your consumption of whole grains? List those ideas below:

_____

_____

2. Jesus was kosher. He ate a wide variety of fresh, clean-species fish. He most likely ate fish that was grilled, baked, broiled, and poached.

We can follow His example, Colbert says, by adding more fish to our diets and by taking fish oil supplements. Colbert warns against eating shellfish (fish that do not have scales, like shrimp and lobster), which he says are "miniature waste collectors for viruses, bacteria, parasites, and toxic waste products."[5] Scripture says that they are an "abomination" to human beings (Lev. 11:12).

Think about your own meal plans for the next two weeks. What can you include to increase your consumption of fish? List those ideas below:

_____

_____

3. Jesus ate clean, kosher meats—free-range animals slaughtered in a biblical way and stripped of excess fat. He ate red meat very sparingly. He also ate poultry.

We can follow His example by choosing free-range and kosher beef and poultry, removing all fat before cooking and cooking our meat products by baking, grilling, or roasting and draining all the fat.[6] He also ate lots and lots of lamb.

Think about your meal plans for the next two weeks. How can you vary them according to Jesus' example? List those ideas below:

_____

_____

4. Jesus ate a diet abundant in vegetables, especially garlic, onions, leeks, beans, and lentils—these vegetables were often a main dish and were routinely enhanced with herbs and spices common to Israel.

We can follow His example by adding more vegetables to our diet and by eating these fresh, whole vegetables raw, lightly steamed, or lightly sautéd in olive oil.[7]

Think about your meal plans for the next two weeks. How can you add more vegetables that are raw, lightly steamed, or lightly sautéd in olive oil? List those ideas below:

_____

_____

5. Jesus ate a great deal of fruit, some nuts, and some honey.

We can follow His example by eating more fresh whole fruit daily, and occasionally treat ourselves to nuts and a little honey mixed into yogurt or drizzled on fruit.[8]

Think about your meal plans for the next two weeks. How can you add more fresh fruit or nuts or honey? List those ideas on the following page:

I highly recommend Don Colbert's book *What Would Jesus Eat?* if you are committed to a healthy lifestyle. As Dr. Colbert says, "If you truly want to follow Jesus in every area of your life, you cannot ignore your eating habits. It is an area in which you can follow Him daily and reap great rewards for doing so. God, in turn, will honor your heartfelt commitment by giving you more energy, better health, and a greater sense of well-being."[9]

I'd like to end this chapter by having you read through the following "Affirmations of a Woman of God."

AFFIRMATIONS OF A WOMAN OF GOD

I am a beautiful woman of God.
I am a capable, intelligent, and virtuous woman.
I am far more precious than jewels and
My value is far above rubies and pearls.
Strength and dignity are my clothing and
My position is strong and secure.
I open my mouth with skillful and godly wisdom.
The bread of idleness, gossip, discontent, and self-pity I will not eat.
The beauty of this world is vain,
But my beauty comes from reverently fearing the Lord.
Each day I will focus on the present, knowing that
God's grace is sufficient for every task.
I surrender all disappointments, fears, and misunderstandings to the Lord,

Forgetting those things which are behind, and
Laying aside every sin and weight that easily entangle me,
I press on to the high prize of being a woman of God.
I am strong in You, Lord, and in the power of Your might.
God, You are my Father and I am Your precious daughter.
Jesus, You are my bridegroom and I am Your beautiful bride.
I am created in Your image, a picture of Your love.
I am a beautiful woman of God.

chapter thirteen

Blessed and Highly Favored:

Walking in Divine Blessing

"For You, O LORD, will bless the righteous; with favor You will sur-round him as with a shield."

—PSALM 5:12

Throughout Scripture women have been blessed and highly favored by God. The God of Abraham, Isaac, and Jacob has set women apart with a special anointing to bring the good news to this dark world. God showed favor to Sarah by giving her Isaac, the son of the covenant, a covenant that still stands with His chosen people to this day. God showed favor to Ruth through Boaz, the husband who brought her into the line of the Messiah. Her son, Obed, became the grandfather of King David. God showed favor to Esther as she saved her people from annihilation in Persia. God showed favor to Mary by allowing her to carry our Lord and Savior within her womb. Bishop T.D. Jakes says that Mary was the only woman to carry the Lord twice, once in her womb and once in her spirit when she received Him in the Upper Room. And God showed favor to Phoebe, the radiant one, who carried Paul's important letter to the church at Rome. Think of it, the God who created the universe and holds us in the palm of His hand chose a woman to take the life-changing gospel to the nations of the world!

Every daughter of the King is chosen to shine for the Lord in the world today. We are to exhibit His glory so brilliantly that people will come from far and near, just to see the Shekinah glory of God within us.

In this chapter we will look at the unmerited favor of God, the ways that each of us walks in divine blessing. King David saw God's favor in his life. He said, "For You, O LORD, will bless the righteous; with favor You will surround him as with a shield" (Ps. 5:12).

Some people equate the unmerited favor of God with prosperity. And prosperity is then equated with financial provision. Even though financial provision is part of the favor of God, His favor encompasses much more than that. The Hebrew translation of the word *prosperity* is safety, wellness, happiness, healthiness, and peacefulness. God wants to prosper us in all these areas.

Before I was saved I had no problem believing that God was a God of blessings; I just had trouble believing these blessings were for me. I saw God as a distant figure. He was too busy with the major problems in the world—the starving children in Third World countries and the soldiers who are dying as they fight for freedom—to even know my name. I rejoiced when I saw Him give gifts and blessings to others. Yet I never expected Him to give me anything. I felt I did not deserve His love or His gifts.

A story inspired by one in the *The Prayer of Jabez* illustrates how wrong I was. A man is touring heaven and he comes to the room with a door marked with his name. Curious, he asks the angel, "What is behind the door?" The angel opens the door and shows him a room full of beautiful presents wrapped in gorgeous paper with gold and silver ribbons. These lavish gifts are stacked to the ceiling! They are breathtaking!

"Who are these gifts for?" the man asks.

"They were yours," the angel answers.

"Mine?" the man surprisingly responds.

"Yes. These were the gifts you never accepted from the Lord. He prepared them for you and wanted to give them to you to bless you and favor you, but you never received them."

Instantly I knew this man was me! The Lord had offered me beautiful, invaluable gifts that I had refused to accept because I did not feel worthy. What had I done?

I thought of how excited I get when I find the perfect gift for my husband or my children. How I wrap this perfect gift with expectation. How I can hardly wait for John or my children to open this gift. I imagine the kind of response they will have; I delight in the fact that I will bring them joy with my gift. How heartbroken I would be if they refused to accept my gift, especially if they did not think they deserved it. I had done that very thing. I had refused to accept the bountiful gifts the Lord had prepared for me. I had broken the Lord's heart.

I wept. I asked the Lord to forgive me for the many times I had refused to accept His love gifts. From that day forward I vowed that I would open every gift the Lord had for me. Then, when I get to heaven, the room with my name on the door will be filled with opened boxes and beautiful wrapping paper and gold and silver ribbon scattered all over the floor as evidence that all my gifts had been gladly received! I now seek to receive all that God has for me on this earth.

I know that the God of this universe answers our cries for help with His favor and wants to give us what our hearts desire. When our daughter Tina was a little girl, she would often say, "Look at me, Daddy!" She knew her father would be pleased with her. She knew her father would see her accomplishments. Our *Jehovah Shammah* is the God who sees. When Hagar was alone in the wilderness she cried out to Him and He answered her. Scripture tells us that "thereafter, Hagar referred to the LORD, who had spoken to her, as 'the God who sees me,' for she said, 'I have seen the One who sees me!'" (Gen. 16:13 NLT).

It is important to remember one very significant fact when we read of the favor and protection the Lord provided for Hagar: She was an unbeliever. I often look back at my life and see the hand of a loving God upon me before I was saved. Even then His protection, His direction, and His unmerited favor could be traced in my life. How much more does He provide now that I am His and have proclaimed Him as my Lord and Savior? He provides my all.

Take time to list the occasions you know God's hand has been on your life even before you accepted Him as Savior.

_____

_____

_____

Thankfully the Lord provides His unmerited favor to us.

GOD'S UNMERITED FAVOR

Take a walk with me through the pages of the Old Testament and see how God's favor is pervasive for His children. God's favor promises . . .

1. Salvation and Joy

Psalm 106:4–5 says, "Remember me, O LORD, with the favor You have toward Your people. Oh, visit me with Your salvation, that I may see the benefit of Your chosen ones, that I may rejoice in the gladness of Your nation, that I may glory with Your inheritance."

If you had a relative who gave all to you at the time of his death, and all you had to do was go to his lawyer's office to accept your inheritance, which was worth an unbelievable sum of wealth, would you go? Or would you refuse to go because you didn't think you were worthy? Would you expect the lawyers to find someone needier than you? I think not!

To receive our Father's inheritance, which is valued far above what man can measure, we need to visit the Cross of our Advocate, Jesus Christ, and accept what has already been prepared for us: eternal life and unmerited favor.

The Lord's unmerited favor begins with the Cross and our salvation. Salvation is a free gift given to us by a righteous God. Paul told the Roman Christians: "Since God did not spare even his own Son but gave him up for us all, won't God, who gave us Christ, also give us everything else?" (Rom. 8:32 NLT).

I have given you many opportunities to accept the Lord into your life within the pages of this book and the book *The King's Daughter*. If you have not accepted the Lord Jesus Christ into your life, please consider doing so now. Seal your salvation by praying the following prayer of salvation:

> *Lord, I ask that You forgive me of all my sins, both known and unknown. I ask that You accept me as Your own and write my name in the Lamb's Book of Life. From this day forward I will read Your Word and obey it. Because of the blood of the Cross, I am now forgiven. My sins are buried in the sea of forgetfulness, never to be remembered against me anymore. I am now a child of God, the daughter of the King, and Jesus Christ is the Lord of my life. Amen.*

If you have already accepted Him into your life, then I ask you to consider saying a prayer of rededication if you feel you do not have God's favor in your life:

> *Lord, I ask that You forgive me of all the transgressions I have committed against You and Your Word. I repent of the sin that has kept me from Your favor. From this day forward I will read Your Word and I will commit myself to You as the source of all my blessings and favor. Amen.*

God's favor also promises . . .

2. Supernatural Increase and Promotion

Genesis 39:21 says, "But the LORD was with Joseph and showed him mercy, and He gave him favor in the sight of the keeper of the prison."

J. Vernon McGee notes that "the interesting thing is that the Lord is with Joseph. Although He does not appear to him, as He had to the other patriarchs, He shows him mercy. First He causes the keeper of the prison to like him and to trust him. Although Joseph is naturally a very attractive young man and has tremendous ability, yet the important thing to note is that all of this would have come to naught had not God been with him. God is with him and is leading him. All of these experiences are moving toward the accomplishment of a purpose in this young man's life.

"Joseph recognized this, and it gave him a buoyancy, an attitude of optimism. The circumstances did not get him down. He lived on top of his circumstances. I have a preacher friend who tells me my problem is that the circumstances are all on top of me! I think many of us live that way. But Joseph was one who was living on top of his circumstances. The Lord was with him. He recognized the hand of God in his life, and so he was not discouraged."[1]

Twice in the last chapters of Genesis, Joseph gives God the glory for his supernatural increase and promotion. When the king's butler and the baker who are imprisoned with Joseph ask for an interpretation of their dreams, Joseph replies, "Do not interpretations belong to God?" (Gen. 40:8). And later when Pharaoh says to Joseph, "I have heard it said of you that you can understand a dream, to interpret it," Joseph replies, "It is not in me; God will give Pharaoh an answer of peace" (Gen. 41:15–16).

J. Vernon McGee wants all Christians to understand the necessity of giving glory to God when He shows favor upon them. McGee says, "Joseph gives God all the glory in this. . . . I wish Christians today would do this. . . . I believe that one of the reasons many of us are not blessed as much as the Lord would like to bless us is because when we do receive something wonderful, we take it for granted and we do not give God the glory for it."[2]

Think about your own life. Has God given you supernatural increase and promotion? If so, mention those ways in the space below:

_____

_____

_____

_____

If not, then list those areas in your life or the life of a loved one where you desire God's supernatural increase and promotion in the space below:

_____

_____

_____

God's favor also promises . . .

3. Restoration of Everything the Enemy Has Stolen from You

Exodus 3:21 says, "And I will give this people favor in the sight of the Egyptians; and it shall be, when you go, that you shall not go empty-handed."

God allows the Israelites to take silver and gold and clothing from the Egyptians who amazingly don't seem to object. Here the Lord is giving the Hebrew slaves the back wages they deserve for several hundred years work.

And the Lord promises to restore everything the enemy has stolen from each of us. You will remember Dupe Adedeji, the young Nigerian woman who married an American citizen and came to the United States. Dupe told me about the plight of widows in Nigeria. When a man pays a woman's dowry and marries her, she becomes part of his property. Then if that man dies before his wife, the man's family takes everything from the widow and throws her out on the street. If the woman doesn't have a good job or a good family, she ends up with nothing.

"A woman who worked with me at a bank in Nigeria took out a loan to build a house for her and her husband," Dupe said. "The loan had both of their names on it, just as most mortgages in the United States. Six months after their house was finished, her husband died.

"This woman's brother-in-law broke the news about her husband's death to her. Then he immediately said, 'You need to move out of the house.'

"'No. I built this house,' she said. 'You know I did.'

"'That doesn't make any difference,' her brother-in-law replied. 'The house belongs to my brother and therefore it belongs to our family.' He kicked this woman out of her own home, and she has not lived there since, even though she is still required to pay the loan on the house."

Abundance Ministries reaches out to these widows to restore what the enemy has stolen from them. The ministry gives them money for food and teaches them a trade, such as tie-dyeing fabric for clothes or making bead necklaces or making soaps and pomades (hair lotions). The courses last for three months; once a woman signs up for the course, she must attend all the sessions. At the end of these courses, the ministry holds a graduation ceremony and exhibits the items these women have made. Then Abundance gives the women seed money to set up their own businesses.

Through Abundance Ministries the Lord is redeeming what the enemy has stolen.

Think about your life. Has God redeemed what the enemy has stolen? Mention some ways in the space below:

_____

_____

_____

_____

If not, watch for God's favor in this way in your life or the life of a loved one in the future. In fact I want you to do more than watch, I want you to anticipate. If you cannot list those things that God has redeemed for you, then list that which you want redeemed. Make sure all of the things you desire are in accordance with the Word of God and believe that He meant what He said in His Word. Then wait with anticipation as He answers your prayer.

_____

_____

_____

God's favor also promises . . .

4. Great Victories in the Midst of Impossible Odds

In the Old Testament King Jehoshaphat faced an invasion from many enemies, the Moabites, the Ammonites, and other nations. Even a king who was favored by God feared the coming battle. So he asked his people to join him in prayer and fasting. God answered their prayers in this way: "Listen, all you of Judah and you inhabitants of Jerusalem, and you, King Jehoshaphat! Thus says the LORD to you: 'Do not be afraid nor dismayed because of this great multitude, for the battle is not yours, but God's'" (2 Chr. 20:15).

With this promise in mind, Jehoshaphat organized an unusual army. "He appointed those who should sing to the LORD, and who should praise the beauty of holiness, as they went out before the army. . . . Now when they began to sing and to praise, the LORD set ambushes against the people of Ammon, Moab, and Mount Seir who had come against Judah; and they were defeated" (2 Chr. 20:21–22).

As King Jehosphat organized his army to sing praises unto the Lord so our church comes together once a quarter and has a night of praise and worship. We call these services "The Night of Extravagant Praise." My husband often says that "the first sermon our members hear every Sunday comes from the choir and musicians."

However, these nights are different. Thousands of people come together as our choir and orchestra present God's Word in songs of praise, just as David sang before the God of his salvation. The service begins with the sound of the *Shofar* calling the congregation to praise. The banners of the Lord are presented as a reminder of His infinite provision for His people. Then we begin to praise the Lord for all that He has done for us. This thunderous praise then turns into sweet worship as we tell God who He is in our lives. He is our Savior. He is our Provider. He is our Healer. He is our Deliverance. He is our Restoration. He is our All.

Children sing and dance unto the Lord, sensing the purity of the service as they watch their parents weep with sincerity. A holy hush enters in the presence of the Holy Spirit as the sweet aroma of praise and worship reaches the throne of the living God. My husband describes this time as "feeling the flutter of angel wings." The Holy Spirit truly stands amidst His people.

When we began having The Night of Extravagant Praise, our services lasted one hour. Now they last at least two hours as men and women humble themselves at the altar. Even after the services come to a close, the youth continue to rejoice until they fulfill their desire to praise the God of their salvation.

Members of our congregation know that this time of praise and worship is a divine appointment with their awesome God. Nothing is more important than His presence in our lives!

Through worship and praise God gave Jehoshaphat victory in the midst of impossible odds.

And He promises the same victory to us today. Many people can testify to this. Warren Beemer, our youth minister at Cornerstone, and his wife, Susan, have seen God's favor in their lives, despite impossible odds.

The couple got married in 1989, when Warren was nineteen years old and

Susan was seventeen. They decided to wait a while before they had children, so Susan took birth control pills. When she went to the doctor for a regular checkup in September of 1990, the doctor asked her, "When was your last period?"

Susan thought for a while, then said, "I haven't had one for two months."

"Have you done a pregnancy test?"

"No, I haven't. I haven't even thought about taking one." Susan just thought she'd skipped a period or so.

"Well, let's do a test right now."

Once the doctor returned to the examining room, he said, "The test was positive."

Susan was amazed. And so was Warren when he heard the news.

"Come back in two weeks," the doctor said, "and we will listen for the baby's heartbeat."

Two weeks later, as the nurse was examining Susan, she said, "When the doctor comes in we should hear a heartbeat."

Soon the doctor placed the ultrasound on Susan's stomach. It wasn't long before he said, "There's no heartbeat." The doctor then told Susan she might not be as far along as he had previously thought. He did an internal exam and said that the child should be about the size of a grapefruit. "Since the baby isn't, you will miscarry. Let's wait and see what happens. When you begin spotting and cramping, we'll do a D and C. Don't worry about this. It's not unusual for women to miscarry during their first pregnancy."

However, the next years proved that Susan did have reason to worry. She became pregnant in July of 1991, but the ultrasound did not show a heartbeat. Again she miscarried.

Two months later, she became pregnant and miscarried for the third time. In the fall of 1991, the Beamers moved from North Carolina to Baton Rouge so Warren could serve as a youth pastor in a church there.

By January of 1992, Susan was again pregnant. During this ultrasound Susan could see the form of a baby, but the ultrasound again failed to show a heartbeat. The new doctor asked, "Have your previous doctors done any testing?"

"No," Susan replied. "They did inquire about my family history—about my mother and grandmother's pregnancies. But they haven't done any tests."

"Since this is your fourth miscarriage, I'd like to have specialists fly in from New York City to Women's Hospital in Baton Rouge to see what the problem is," the doctor said. "We'll do blood work on you and your husband, and I'll take blood from the placenta when I give you a D and C."

The Beemers were relieved to hear that specialists would try to resolve their problem.

But the prognosis was not good. "Your husband's blood work was okay. His chromosomes are perfectly fine," the doctor said. "However, your DNA test was not good. Your reproductive chromosomes—9 and 18, which are a pair—are defective." The doctor paused to give Susan and Warren an opportunity to deal with this fact.

Then he continued. "This means that you, Susan, have a 75 percent chance of having a handicapped child, and you only have a 25 percent chance of carrying a child to term. I recommend that you and your husband adopt children. It's almost impossible for you to have a normal child."

Susan couldn't believe what the doctor had said. She was just twenty-one, Warren was twenty-three, and they'd been told they would probably not have children. Their hopes for a family seemed to be destroyed. Yet the couple rejected the doctor's advice. We want children, they decided. We will just keep trying— and we will trust God for the future.

When Susan became pregnant in 1993, she again miscarried. In 1994 she miscarried for a sixth time. The sack was empty. *It's me!* Susan thought. *I'm the problem. Warren could have children if he wasn't married to me.*

Susan again became pregnant in February of 1996. That month her grandfather had a heart attack so she went home to see him. Again she started to spot and experience cramping. Because the baby was about twelve weeks, her cervix dilated and the cramping felt like what Susan expected of labor pains.

That September the Beemers moved to San Antonio so Warren could serve as our youth pastor. I knew about Susan's past history, and I recommended that she see my brother-in-law, Dr. Scott Farhart.

As Dr. Farhart looked over the Beemers' records he explained that Susan's problem was that she had more bad eggs than good ones. He told the Beemers, "We need to start praying for a good egg."

At the end of their initial visit, Scott said, "We're not going to do any more testing. We know what the tests say. . . . But we also know what God can do."

Susan told me she was relieved to have a Christian doctor who would pray and believe with them. Before the Beemers left the office, Scott again said, "Remember, we know what God can do."

In 1998 Susan again became pregnant and both the Beemers and Scott were excited. Susan thought, *This is it! God has answered our prayers.*

But as Scott did the ultrasound she could see the disappointment in his eyes. There was no heartbeat. She had miscarried for the eighth time.

After Scott left the examining room, Susan looked at Warren. "I can't handle this anymore," she said. "My body just can't stand this routine again—becoming pregnant, waiting patiently for the ultrasound, and not having anything there. You might as well put me in Laurel Ridge."

Susan had reached a desperate point in her life; she was not exaggerating when she suggested that she might need some time in a mental health facility. Still she cried out to God, *I know You have a plan for my life. I've served You, God. I haven't lived an ungodly life, but still I am going through this horrible situation. Please, God, help me to understand what You are doing.*

Yes, Susan questioned God, but she never stopped believing that God did not make a mistake. In fact, she told me, "Knowing that God had a plan for my life is what carried me through those eight miscarriages. I know God has a plan."

Before the couple left his office, Scott told Susan, "I'll give you a D and C so you have a clean womb, and we'll talk about this later."

The next week she returned for a checkup and Scott again said, "We need to start praying for a good egg."

As Susan and her husband drove down Highway 281 after the appointment, she cried out to God, *Lord, this is it. If You never give me a child, I'll still serve You. But I'm going to get pregnant one more time. Please help me to carry this child. I can't continue to go through miscarriages. I believe You gave me the desire to have children, and I'm holding onto that in faith.*

In December of 1999 Susan attended a breakfast I held for my twelve Esther ladies and the twelve women who are co-leaders with their husbands of John's Government of Twelve. Susan told me she almost didn't come. And as she drove to the church she brought her doubts before the Lord. *God, I just need You to speak to me. I need You to tell me I should be under this leadership, that I am worthy to be one of Diana's Esther women. I feel so unworthy as a woman. I can't carry a child as most women do. Show me Your will at this luncheon.*

After the meal, the women began to pray for me. As Karen Park was praying, she stopped abruptly and said, "Susan Beemer, God has a word for you."

At first Susan reacted with apprehension. She had forgotten about her plea for God's guidance and wondered what Karen would say.

"Susan," Karen continued, "the desire of your heart is going to be fulfilled. The promise God has made for you is going to come true."

Those were the words that Susan had hoped to hear for so long. Two weeks later, in January of 2000 Susan knew she was again pregnant. *I'm not going to take another pregnancy test,* she decided. *I've spent too much money on them already.*

Instead she made an appointment to see Dr. Farhart. That day as she was sitting in his office she was all too aware of the many pregnant women sitting around her. *Oh, God, I just can't take another disappointment. I need to know that*

I'm going to be a mother. I need to know that You are in control. I need to know that Your will is being done.

Before the test, the Beemers prayed for God's will as they had many times before. Then they watched as Scott began the ultrasound. The familiar picture of the womb came up on the screen. "Let's see if we can see the heartbeat," Scott said. As he moved the probe around, the Beemers saw the flutter of a heartbeat after eleven years of waiting.

This is it, Susan thought. *My miracle child! This baby's going to make it. This baby is a fighter.*

And Susan did carry her first child, Susan Abagail (which means "my father's joy") to term. She was in labor for twenty-one hours, but she told me, "I loved every minute of it, and I loved every minute of my pregnancy. God's hand was in it."

Susan Abagail Beemer is a beautiful, smart little girl, exactly the opposite of the handicapped child the doctor had foreseen in 1992. And God gave the Beemers a second daughter in 2002: Kaitlyn Renee.

When Susan remembers those eleven years, during which she experienced eight miscarriages, she says, "Looking back, the pain of the past isn't there anymore. God removed it. If I had to go through those eight miscarriages all over again to have my girls, I'd do it. It was more than worth it. When you submit your life to God, He turns your greatest tragedies into His greatest triumphs."

God gave the Beemers victory in the midst of impossible odds.

Think about your life. Has God given you a victory in the midst of impossible odds? If so, describe that experience in the space below:

_____

_____

_____

_____

If not, list those victories that cannot be provided by man but can only be achieved by God's supernatural intervention. Be specific with your list. John tells our congregation that we must be specific when we list our petitions before the Lord. If your child needs a bicycle, then list a red bicycle with training wheels and yellow racing stripes. When you get your provision you will know it came from God!

_____

_____

_____

God's favor also promises . . .

5. Petitions Granted

God's favor on Esther enabled her to represent her people, the downtrodden and persecuted Jews, to King Ahasuerus.

Esther asked Ahasuerus, "If it pleases the king, and if I have found favor in his sight . . ., let it be written to revoke the letters devised by Haman, the son of Hammedatha the Agagite, which he wrote to annihilate the Jews who are in all the king's provinces" (Esther 8:5).

Even though Esther was the queen of Persia, she could not approach the king unless he acknowledged her by lowering his golden scepter. If Ahasuerus didn't do so, and Esther still approached him, she would be killed. Yet the king answered her petition and agreed to revoke the decree to annihilate the Jews. King Ahasuerus directed Esther and her uncle, Mordecai: "You yourselves write a decree concerning the Jews, as you please, in the king's name, and seal it with the king's signet ring; for whatever is written in the king's name and sealed with the king's signet ring no one can revoke" (Esther 8:8).

Without God's favor this would never have been possible. Imagine Adolf

Hitler agreeing to shut down the Nazi concentration camps during the Second World War. That's an analogy to what occurred so many years ago in Persia.

And our God promises such favor to us today.

My husband and I have had many impossible petitions granted on our behalf throughout our ministry, like the one that occurred in 2004 when Dupe Adedeji and her husband, Diran, returned to Ibadan, a former capital of the western providence of Nigeria. On these trips the Adedejis always visit a local orphanage that houses about fifty children. They go there every other week when they are in Nigeria to take the children food and clothing and to see if any child needs medical care. It's not unusual for the children to be malnourished and to develop malaria or typhoid.

On August 4, Diran, Dupe, Warren Beemer, Teresa Hall, Christina Natalina, and some Abundance Ministries staff members arrived at the state-run orphanage, a small complex of several concrete, faded-blue buildings with no electricity and no running water. The Adedejis had not called ahead and intentionally arrived at the orphanage early in the morning so they could see how the children were really being kept.

Diran said, "The first thing that hits you when you arrive at the orphanage is the foul smell of urine and feces. Since the orphanage does not have any restrooms, the nearby bush is used as a refuge dump."

Once inside the first building Diran introduced the team to the orphanage staff. "They welcomed us in words," Diran said, "but their demeanor showed that we were really not welcome without advance notice."

As Diran walked through the orphanage he noticed a young preteen girl he didn't recognize who was playing cards with a younger child whom Diran had seen several times before. He approached the children and heard the older girl speaking English with an American accent.

Curious, he asked one of the staff members, "Who is that girl? Does she live here?"

The woman answered, "No, she lives somewhere around here. She's just come to visit." The woman was unusually vague.

Since this staff member seemed to resist any further questioning, Diran continued into the second building. Soon he found another girl and a boy he also didn't recognize, sitting on the floor, talking to each other. So Diran asked the girl, "How are you?"

And the girl replied, "Good."

That one statement and the girl's heavy American accent told Diran the girl was also not from Nigeria. Native Nigerians typically answer "fine" to the question "How are you?"

Curious, he asked the girl, "Where are you from?"

"Texas," she answered.

"Texas!?" I'm from Texas too. . . . What part of Texas?"

"Houston."

"I'm from San Antonio," Diran replied. "What in the world are you doing here?"

"My mother brought us to Nigeria; then she left us here."

Diran was shocked and he began asking other questions. "How many American children are here?" The answer: seven. "How long have you been here?" About a week and a half.

The girl, whose name was Brandy, led Diran and the rest of the team to the room where she and the other six American children lived, a small filthy room that had no windows. The children slept on the bare floor in this damp room. They all looked malnourished and unkempt. One complained of being sick.

Diran and the team members were amazed. Here were seven American children, born in a free country that promised them every opportunity, now abandoned in the middle of Africa, far away from all they had known. The children had scabs from mosquito bites and one was covered with festering sores from impetigo, a skin disease that results from a filthy infection.

Tears came to the team's eyes as they learned why the children, who ranged in age from eight to sixteen, had been sequestered in this orphanage. Their foster mother had brought them to Nigeria in October of 2003, under the pretext of taking them on holiday to Germany. She was engaged to a Nigerian man, who had recommended the boarding schools there as a safe place for the children while she trained and worked as a civilian food-service contractor in Iraq. She stayed with the children for about one month and then returned to America for her training, leaving the seven children in the care of a Nigerian man whom they called uncle. She had promised to send money for their support, and at first she did so. But soon the money stopped coming, even though the mother was receiving in excess of $3,500 to offset their care from social services. Then the man abandoned the children.

In the next weeks the neighbors noticed the children wandering the neighborhood and begging for food. Since the area was unsafe—less than a mile from there a man had been arrested for carrying a sack containing body parts of an elderly man and the torso of a decapitated and emasculated infant—the neighbors began helping the children who were obviously alone in the ramshackle two-story house. They also enlisted the help of some churches. However, after awhile this became too much of a burden for both the neighbors and the churches. The neighbors called the social welfare department who took the seven children to the orphanage.

That bright and sunny morning on August 4, the Abundance team members promised the children they would be going home. But the seven hungry children would not believe them. They had told their story so many times to so many other people and nothing had happened. They seemed hard and calloused from almost ten months of misery, living in a foreign land where they had been abandoned and then taken to this orphanage.

The team members tried to encourage the seven sickly children. And they did cheer up as the ministry team talked to them about the Dallas Cowboys and

Houston Rockets center Yao Ming. The children even jeered when Warren mentioned the Los Angeles Lakers, and they clapped when he told them Shaquille O'Neal had been traded to the Miami Heat.

The team decided to turn to my husband for help. Warren Beamer took all the information and put it in an email to Pastor Hagee. After he received the email, my husband called Warren in Nigeria and asked him if he was sure of the information. Warren replied, "Pastor, I'm looking at seven American children in harm's way."

At first John was astonished and wondered if the children were really from Houston. But Warren said, "The seven kids know too much about Rockets center Yao Ming and their church's bus ministry to be anything but true Houstonians."

After talking to my husband, the Abundance Ministries staff members photographed the children. Dupe also had them write their names on notepads, and Warren Beemer left a one-dollar bill with the children. He told them that when they got back to America he would trade it for a one-hundred dollar bill. Warren then led the children in the national anthem.

Upon confirming that the information was accurate, John phoned U.S. Senator John Cornyn, R-Texas, whom he'd met when Cornyn was running for the Texas Supreme Court in 1990. He also called House Majority Leader Tom DeLay, R-Sugar Land, who had spoken at Cornerstone's annual "Night to Honor Israel."

The congressmen and their staffs then contacted the U.S. State Department, and three days later, after much deliberation through phone calls and faxes, the children were moved to the U.S. Embassy in Nigeria. Within one week the seven American children were out of that orphanage and on their way back to the states. "For the United States government, that was lighting speed," my husband said.

God had favored these young boys and girls, and our petitions on behalf of these children had been granted.

God also promises that our petitions will be answered.

Think about your life. Has God allowed your petitions to be answered?

Describe one experience in the space below:

_____

_____

_____

_____

We have heard the Word of the Lord. We must believe the Word for our lives. He extends His favor to all of us. All we must do is believe, ask, and receive.

BELIEVE, ASK, AND RECEIVE

The first step in experiencing God's favor is to believe that God is your Father. You must not only believe that He is Your Father, you must know that you are His daughter and deserve His blessings.

From 2002–2004 we were in a faith walk. Our home of years was declared unhealthy because of black mold infestation. For two years all our belongings were in twenty-seven crates at a storage facility.

The five of us moved from our home of eighteen years to a hotel for eight weeks and from that hotel we went to an apartment for over eight months and from that apartment to a rental home for one full year. We were out of the sanctuary of our home for two full years.

Not all of those days were good ones. But I knew God was my Father and I was His daughter. I knew I belonged to the God who owns the cattle on a thousand hills. And I knew to ask for His help.

WE MUST ASK

I know that the Word says that we have not because we ask not so I asked God to either return our home to us in better condition than ever before or give us a new home. Our God is *Jehovah Jirah,* the Lord our provider. He will provide for His own.

John and I learned that possessions even though given by God are not important in our lives. Family is. We learned that no matter what dwelling we lived in, we were content to be together and healthy. We laughed at the unusual circumstances we were in, often to keep from crying. Nonetheless, we knew God was in control.

During this time the Lord brought many new friends into our lives who would help us through the tough moments. And many long-time friends also stood with us. Even the insurance company showed us favor. When our lawyer met with us, he said, "Diana and John, I am astonished at how well the insurance company treated you."

We were happy to receive God's favor.

RECEIVE

I am now writing to you from my husband's study. I can hear workmen in my kitchen and on the front porch of our home, still restoring it to working order. We are together, we are healthy, and we are happy and grateful for all the Lord has done and continues to do on our behalf for He is good and He is faithful. We are walking in His divine blessing and favor.

In our Woman of God classes we make proclamations of God's favor over our lives from His Word in the Bible.

PROCLAMATIONS

We believe the proclamations in the Word of God are true. We believe these proclamations of favor are for each one of us, not because we have earned them with works, but because they are gifts of unconditional and unmerited favor from our Father.

Repeat this proclamation after me to claim your possession as a daughter of the King:

In the name of Jesus, I am the righteousness of God; therefore I am entitled to covenant kindness and favor. The favor of God is among the righteous. His favor surrounds the righteous; therefore it surrounds me. Everywhere I go, everything I do, I expect the favor of God to be in manifestation. Never again will I be without the favor of God.

Satan, my days in Lodebar cease today. I am leaving that place of lack and want. I am going from the pit to the palace because the favor of God is on me. God's favor rests richly on me. God's favor profusely abounds in me, and I am part of the generation that will experience the favor of God, immeasurable, limitless, and surpassing.

Therefore, God's favor produces in my life supernatural increase, promotion, prominence, preferential treatment, restoration, honor, increased assets, great victories, recognition, petitions granted, policies and rules changed on my behalf, and battles won that I don't have to fight. The favor of God is upon me, His favor goes before me, and therefore my life will never be the same again. Amen.

We have just proclaimed blessings for ourselves that some of us never thought possible over our lives. It is time we begin to live in the inheritance our Heavenly Father has so freely given us.

We must begin to think like the King's daughters.

We must being to act like the King's daughters.

We must begin to live like the King's daughters.

Once we do, we will never be the same again.

For whoever finds me finds life,
And obtains favor from the Lord.

—Proverbs 8:35

part two

A Curriculum
for
Women's Groups

The Purpose of the Journey:

Beginning Steps

*W*elcome to the study guides for your Woman of God curriculum. Esther's God-given destiny for her life was revealed when her Uncle Mordecai challenged her to save the people she loved with theses prophetic words " . . . Yet who knows whether you have come to the kingdom for such a time as this" (Esth. 4:14).

The moment she put others before herself, she discovered her destiny. From the beginning of time God appointed her to become a queen, an intercessor, and a deliverer of a nation. However, before she could accomplish God's purposes in her life she had to prepare herself, and that's the intent of these sessions: preparation.

We have been praying according to Colossians 1:9–10 that we will be filled with the knowledge of God's will in all wisdom and spiritual understanding, walking worthy of the Lord, fully pleasing Him, being fruitful in every good work and increasing in the knowledge of God, being strengthened with all might, according to His glorious power for all patience and longsuffering with joy.

This curriculum has been designed with that Scripture in mind. It is with great *expectation that we share our lives and God's vision with you. My goal is to assist you in your journey. You are a daughter of the King, a beautiful unique work of love.*

These sessions are not intended to be just another Bible study; this is an interactive journey. Our desire is to equip and encourage you to become the woman God designed you to be. The joy and challenge of this experience will be shared with your sisters in Christ as we all walk the road of becoming women of God.

I would like to remind you that these sessions are created so we can hear what the Lord has to say to each one of us. Sometimes we think of God in such casual and familiar terms that we forget who He is. Hebrews 12:29 tells us "For our God is a consuming fire." We don't want to be so formal and legalistic that we think we need to have an appointment to meet God, yet we need to remember that He is holy. Everything about Him is holy. We need to separate ourselves from the busyness of this life to seek His holiness. One way is to come before Him in reverence and love, seeking Him, not our loved ones or conversation from friends or advice from counselors, but His profound presence.

Be blessed and allow the Lord to enlarge your territory. I pray for each one of you.

LESSON OBJECTIVES

These sessions were designed to help you develop the critical skills you need to follow in God's direction and leading. Each lesson is designed to equip you with God's knowledge, wisdom, and spiritual understanding. The overall lesson objectives are:

- To understand your value in God's eyes.
- To understand how to live a Christ-like life.
- To understand how to walk in the Spirit in a moment-by-moment experience.
- To participate in writing your personal testimony.
- To understand what God has planned for your life.
- To align your goals with God's will for your life.
- To comprehend your role in the workplace.
- To use prayer and fasting as a guideline in your life.
- To understand how to receive the favor of God.
- To memorize Scripture.

At the beginning of each lesson you will find a Scripture or Scriptures from which the lesson is taken. Read these Scriptures aloud as you begin the group sessions.

One final recommendation: honesty. Please use these lessons as a private and personal journal, expressing your innermost fears, insecurities, hopes, and desires.

PARTICIPATION AGREEMENT

I, _____, agree to do the following in
my group sessions:

1. Participate in all group sessions unless urgent circumstances
   beyond my control prevent my attendance. When unable to
   attend, I will write a paper on the topic discussed and turn it in
   at the next session.

2. Keep all personal matters shared by others in the group confidential.

3. Remember the sanctuary is where we come together to meet God.
   I will come in and take my seat with an attitude of prayer and reverence.

4. Bring no food or drink into the sanctuary.

5. Turn off my pager and/or cell phone.

6. Show respect to others at all times.

7. Will refrain from interrupting when someone else is speaking.

8. Participate openly and honestly in the group sessions.

9. Pray regularly for my fellow group members.

10. Pick up my children immediately after our sessions, and then feel
    free to visit with friends. If someone else is picking up my child, I
    will confirm that my child has been picked up before I leave the
    church property.

Signed:_____ Date:_____

My Facilitation Group

Facilitator Name: Phone#
Address:

1. Name: Phone#
   Address:

2. Name: Phone#
   Address:

3. Name: Phone#
   Address:

4. Name: Phone#
   Address:

5. Name: Phone#
   Address:

6. Name: Phone#
   Address:

7. Name: Phone#
   Address:

8. Name: Phone#
   Address:

9. Name: Phone#
   Address:

As you interact in your small groups, please remember that you are sisters in Christ. Treat each other as Paul suggested in Ephesians 6:18: "praying always with all prayer and supplication in the Spirit, being watchful to this end with all perseverance and supplication for all the saints."

THE FACILITATOR'S ROLE

My facilitator will . . .

- Make announcements for each session.

- Coordinate discussion in small groups.

- Be knowledgeable of godly principles.

- Facilitate our group so we will stay focused.

- Not be a counselor.

- Direct each problem to the Word of God.

- Pray and encourage all members.

◡◠ ASSIGNMENT
_____

Please read Chapter One.

My Value in God's Eyes:

A Lesson on Self-Esteem

"Just as He chose us in Him before the foundation of the world."
—EPHESIANS 1:4

PURPOSE STATEMENT: To discover what it means for you to be God's child
and to know His love, forgiveness, and grace.

LEARNING OBJECTIVES: This session is designed to help you:
1. Understand your sinful nature.
2. Recognize who you are in Christ.
3. Realize you have been created for a purpose.
4. Find freedom from condemnation.
5. Learn to draw close to God.

SCRIPTURE REFERENCES
Ephesians 5:1–2

"Therefore be imitators of God as dear children. And walk in love, as Christ also has loved us and given Himself for us, an offering and a sacrifice to God for a sweet-smelling aroma."

1 Corinthians 15:10

"But by the grace of God I am what I am, and His grace toward me was not in vain; but I labored more abundantly than they all, yet not I, but the grace of God which was with me."

1. Self-esteem: "The Me I See Is the Me I Will Be"

It is important to see yourself as God does. Ask yourself:

- Do I see myself as ugly?

    —This can represent low self-esteem.

- Do I feel unworthy?

    —This can represent rejection in your childhood or now.

- Do I often feel angry?

    —This can represent self-hatred and self-condemnation.

- Do I feel guilty?

    —This can represent emotional, physical, or sexual abuse.

These emotions identify the self-esteem problem we wrestle with daily. Remember, when we confront the enemy we disarm him. List those things you see as ugly in yourself in the space below:

_____

_____

_____

_____

Compare these thoughts with the Word. Paul told the Ephesians, "I, therefore, the prisoner of the Lord, beseech you to walk worthy of the calling with which you were called, with all lowliness and gentleness, with longsuffering, bearing with one another in love" (Eph. 4:1–2).

Think about what Paul is suggesting here:

Lowliness of mind. "I accept all things that God says about me without argument. It enables me to accept myself."

Meekness. "I accept all of God's dealings with me without resistance or bitterness. It enables me to accept God."

Long-suffering. "I accept all of man's dealings with me without retaliation. It enables me to accept my enemies."

Forbearance. "I accept people with all their faults and differences. It enables me to accept my friends."

Jesus Christ will write our names in the Lamb's Book of Life once we pray the sinner's prayer. Pray the prayer below:

Dear Lord, I have made many mistakes in the past. I have sinned against You and Your Holy Spirit. I am sorry for all I have done. Please forgive me. I accept Jesus Christ as my Savior and ask that You will be with me in the days ahead. Amen.

2. Now list all the things you believe are beautiful about yourself. (Interestingly, this will be more difficult than listing the things you don't like about yourself. Believe me, you are not alone in this.) Please do not omit this step because it may be difficult. Quietly ask the Lord to bring to your mind the traits He sees beautiful in you!

_____

_____

_____

After you have done so, realize that God made everything beautiful in its time. Quote the Scriptures below to yourself when you feel ugly or unworthy or angry or guilty (you might even write them in your Bible):

"I am fearfully and wonderfully made" (Ps. 139:14).

"I have called you by your name; You are Mine" (Is. 43:1).

3. You are now ready to read "A Letter from God"

A Letter from God

When I created the heavens and the earth, I spoke them into being. When I created man, I formed him and breathed life into his nostrils. But you, woman, I fashioned after I breathed the breath of life into Man because your nostrils are too delicate. I allowed a deep sleep to come over him so I could patiently and perfectly fashion you.

Man was put to sleep so that he could not interfere with the creativity. From one bone I fashioned you. I chose the bone that protects man's life. I chose the rib, which protects his heart and lungs and supports him, as you are meant to do.

Around this one bone I shaped you. I modeled you. I created you perfectly and beautifully. Your characteristics are as the rib—strong, yet delicate and fragile. You provide protection for the most delicate organ in man, his heart. His heart is the center of his being; his lungs hold the breath of life.

The rib cage will allow itself to be broken before it will allow damage to the heart. Support man as the rib cage supports the body. You were not taken from his feet, to be under him, nor were you taken from his head, to be above him. You were taken from his side, to stand beside him and be held close to his side.

You are my perfect angel. You are my beautiful little girl. You have grown to be a splendid woman of excellence, and My eyes fill when I see the virtue in your heart. Your eyes—don't change them. Your lips—how lovely when they part in prayer. Your nose, so perfect in form. Your hands, so gentle to touch. I've caressed your face in your deepest sleep; I've held your heart close to Mine.

Of all that lives and breathes, you are the most like Me. Adam walked with Me in the cool of the day, and yet he was lonely. He could not see Me or touch Me. He could only feel Me. So everything I wanted Adam to share and experience with Me, I fashioned in you.

My holiness, My strength, My purity, My love, My protection and support. You are special because you are the extension of Me. Man represents My image—Woman, My emotions. Together, you represent the totality of God.

So, man—treat woman well. Love her, respect her, for she is fragile. In hurting her, you hurt Me. What you do to her, you do to Me. In crushing her, you damage your own heart, the heart of your Father and the heart of her Father.

Woman, support man. In humility, show him the power of emotion I have given you. In gentle quietness, show your strength. In love, show him that you are the rib that protects his inner self.

4. Make this declaration over you and those in your group:

   "I am beautiful, you are beautiful. We have value in God's eyes. We are daughters of the King!"

5. Finally read "Releasing the Word in Your Life."

RELEASING THE WORD IN MY LIFE

Father, in the name of Jesus, I repent of my ignorance of the Word of God. I ask You to forgive me of the foolish things I've prayed.

In Jesus' name, I bind every word that has released the devil or drawn his weapons toward me. I bind every hindering force that I've ever given strength to by the words of my mouth. I break the power of those spiritual forces, in Jesus' name.

Father, in the name of Jesus, I ask You to guide me in wisdom and understanding through the scriptural methods and to set in motion all that's good, pure, perfect, lovely, and of good report.

I covenant with You to pray accurately. I will speak only that which glorifies God. I will let no corrupt communication proceed out of my mouth, but that which is good to edify and minister grace through the hearer. I will not grieve the Holy Spirit of God whereby I'm sealed to the day of Redemption, but I will give glory and honor and praise to the Lord Jesus Christ for all that shall be done.

I thank You, Father, that I am the Body of Christ. The enemy has no power over me. I proclaim that all that is good, all that is blessed of God, all that is in the perfect will of God, all that God has designed for me shall come to me, in Jesus' name.

All of the evil and the bad reports, all that the enemy has designed to deceive me, to lead me astray, to destroy my home, my finances, or me shall be stopped with the name of Jesus and the works of my mouth.

I'm blessed in the city and blessed in the field. I'm blessed in the baskets and blessed in the store. I'm blessed coming in; I'm blessed going out. I'm the head and not the tail.

I'm above and not beneath. I'm blessed of Almighty God, strengthened with all might according to Your glorious power.

The Greater One is in me; He puts me over in life. The Spirit of Truth is in me; He gives me divine wisdom, divine direction, divine understanding of every situation, and every circumstance of life. I have the wisdom of God. I thank You, Father, that the Spirit of God leads me. I have the mind of Christ and the wisdom of God is within me. In Jesus' name. Amen!

❧ ASSIGNMENT

Please read Chapter Two.

Close in prayer:

Lord, forgive me. Help me to see God's beauty in myself and in others. Let me look beyond my limits and see not what I am, but what You designed me to be. Help me to receive the reality of who I am in Christ Jesus. I am a joint heir with Christ Jesus, a daughter of the King, precious and elect, chosen for a purpose. I know that Your Word will not return void, but it shall accomplish what You please. Thank You, Father, I am beautiful. I was created with purpose. You did choose me and You will never leave me! In Jesus' name, I pray. Amen.

I Am Not Ashamed of the Gospel:

The Power of My Testimony

"And they overcame him by the blood of the Lamb and by the word of their testimony."

—Revelation 12:11

PURPOSE STATEMENT:

To realize the power of your testimony and the power it has in influencing others to seek the Lord.

LEARNING OBJECTIVE:

This session is designed to help you:
1. Know the biblical foundation for giving a personal testimony.
2. Know the benefits of preparing and giving a personal testimony.
3. Compose and deliver your personal testimony, using a three-point outline.
4. Believe that once you have been redeemed, you are obligated to redeem others.

SCRIPTURE REFERENCES:

Acts 22:15

"For you will be His witness to all men of what you have seen and heard."

Ephesians 4:21–24

"If indeed you have heard Him and have been taught by Him, as the truth is in Jesus: that you put off, concerning your former conduct, the old man which grows corrupt according to the deceitful lusts, and be renewed in the spirit of your mind, and that you put on the new man which was created according to God, in true righteousness and holiness."

Ephesians 5:1

"Therefore be imitators of God as dear children."

Philippians 3:7–11

"But what things were gain to me, these I have counted loss for Christ.

Yet indeed I also count all things loss for the excellence of the knowledge of Christ Jesus my Lord, for whom I have suffered the loss of all things, and count them as rubbish, that I may gain Christ and be found in Him, not having my own righteousness, which is from the law, but that which is through faith in Christ, the righteousness which is from God by faith; that I may know Him and the power of His resurrection, and the fellowship of His sufferings, being conformed to His death, if, by any means, I may attain to the resurrection from the dead."

INTRODUCTION

1. Read Matthew 10:19–20 aloud.

"But when they deliver you up, do not worry about how or what you should speak. For it will be given to you in that hour what you should speak, for it is not you who speak, but the Spirit of your Father who speaks in you."

2. Even though the Holy Spirit will equip you with the right words at the right time, it is your responsibility to be prepared with your testimony.

A PERSONAL TESTIMONY

The purpose of a personal testimony is to present how you received Christ and how Jesus has affected your life. A personal testimony prepares you to be a witness for Christ. Remember, we are witnesses for Christ the moment we receive Him into our hearts.

In the space below, write why you believe it is important to be a witness for Christ:

_____

_____

_____

_____

The Benefits of a Personal Testimony Are:
- A well-prepared, clearly organized testimony, given in the power of the Holy Spirit, has a direct impact in nearly every witnessing situation.
- A personal testimony provides evidence of God at work in your life.
- A personal testimony is one of your most valuable ministry tools. It is effective in large groups, small groups, and one-on-one situations.
- A personal testimony presents Christ in a clear and positive manner with the hope that all who hear will want to know Him personally. God calls us to be the light of the world: "You are the light of the world. A city that is set on a hill cannot be hidden. Nor do they light a lamp and put it under a basket, but on a lampstand, and it gives light to all who are in the house. Let your light so shine before men, that they may see your good works and glorify your Father in heaven" (Matt. 5:14–16).

Biblical Examples of Personal Testimonies:

1. The testimony of the woman at the well: John 4:39–42

> And many of the Samaritans of that city believed Him because of the word of the woman who testified, "He told me all that I ever did."
>
> So when the Samaritans had come to Him, they urged Him to stay with them; and He stayed there two days.
>
> And many more believed because of His own word.
>
> Then they said to the woman, "Now we believe, not because of what you said, for we have heard for ourselves and know that this is indeed the Christ, the Savior of the world."

2. The blind man's testimony: John 9:24–34

> So they again called the man who was blind, and said to him, "Give God the glory! We know that this Man is a sinner."
>
> He answered and said, "Whether He is a sinner or not I do not know. One thing I know: that though I was blind, now I see."
>
> Then they said to him again, "What did He do to you? How did He open your eyes?"
>
> He answered them, "I told you already, and you did not listen. Why do you want to hear it again? Do you also want to become His disciples?"
>
> Then they reviled him and said, "You are His disciple, but we are Moses' disciples.
>
> "We know that God spoke to Moses; as for this fellow, we do not know where He is from."
>
> The man answered and said to them, "Why, this is a marvelous thing, that you do not know where He is from, and yet He has opened my eyes!

"Now we know that God does not hear sinners; but if anyone is a worshiper of God and does His will, He hears him.

"Since the world began it has been unheard of that anyone opened the eyes of one who was born blind.

"If this Man were not from God, He could do nothing."

They answered and said to him, "You were completely born in sins, and are you teaching us?" And they cast him out.

3. Paul's testimony

Paul's testimony is generally divided into three parts:

Paul's life before Christ: Acts 22:1–5. He described what he thought and did before he became a believer:

"Brethren, and fathers, hear my defense before you now."

And when they heard that he spoke to them in the Hebrew language, they kept all the more silent. Then he said:

"I am indeed a Jew, born in Tarsus of Cilicia, but brought up in this city at the feet of Gamaliel, taught according to the strictness of our fathers' law, and was zealous toward God as you all are today.

"I persecuted this Way to the death, binding and delivering into prisons both men and women, as also the high priest bears me witness, and all the council of the elders, from whom I also received letters to the brethren, and went to Damascus to bring in chains even those who were there, to Jerusalem to be punished."

How Paul became a believer: Acts 22:6–10.

"Now it happened, as I journeyed and came near Damascus at about noon, suddenly a great light from heaven shone around me.

"And I fell to the ground and heard a voice saying to me, 'Saul, Saul, why are you persecuting me?'

"So I answered, 'Who are You, Lord?' And He said to me, 'I am Jesus of Nazareth, whom you are persecuting.'

"Now those who were with me indeed saw the light and were afraid, but they did not hear the voice of Him who spoke to me.

"So I said, 'What shall I do, Lord?' And the Lord said to me, 'Arise and go into Damascus, and there you will be told all things which are appointed for you to do.'"

Paul's life after Christ: Acts 22:12–21. Paul explained how becoming a believer changed his life:

"Then a certain Ananias, a devout man according to the law, having a good testimony with all the Jews who dwelt there, came to me; and he stood and said to me, 'Brother Saul, receive your sight.' And at that same hour I looked up at him.

"Then he said, 'The God of our fathers has chosen you that you should know His will, and see the Just One, and hear the voice of His mouth.

'For you will be His witness to all men of what you have seen and heard.

'And now why are you waiting? Arise and be baptized, and wash away your sins, calling on the name of the Lord.'

"Now it happened, when I returned to Jerusalem and was praying in the temple, that I was in a trance and saw Him saying to me, 'Make haste and get out of Jerusalem quickly, for they will not receive your testimony concerning Me.'

"So I said, 'Lord, they know that in every synagogue I imprisoned and beat those who believe on You.

'And when the blood of Your martyr Stephen was shed, I also was standing by consenting to his death, and guarding the clothes of those who were killing him.'

"Then He said to me, 'Depart, for I will send you far from here to the Gentiles.'"

How to Prepare Your Personal Testimony

1. Ask the Lord to give you wisdom and guidance as you write your testimony.

Scripture says, "If any of you lacks wisdom, let him ask of God, who gives to all liberally and without reproach, and it will be given to him. But let him ask in faith, with no doubting, for he who doubts is like a wave of the sea driven and tossed by the wind" (James 1:5–6).

2. Follow Paul's three-point outline:
   - **Before** I received Christ.
   - **How** I received Christ.
   - **After** I received Christ.

3. Questions to consider as you write your personal testimony:

Before I received Christ:

- What was my life like? What were my attitudes, needs, and problems?

_____

_____

- What did my life revolve around the most? Where did I seek my security or happiness?

_____

_____

- In what way did the world's sources for security, peace of mind, and happiness leave me unfulfilled?

_____

_____

How I received Christ:

- When was the first time I heard the gospel? How? (When was I exposed to the truth of God's Word?)

_____

_____

- What were my initial reactions?

_____

_____

- When did my attitude begin to change? How?

_____

_____

- What were the final struggles that went through my mind just before I accepted Christ?

_____

_____

• Even though there were struggles, why did I decide to accept Christ?

_____

_____

After I received Christ:

• What are some specific changes Christ has made in my life, actions, and attitudes?

_____

_____

• How long before I noticed the changes?

_____

_____

• How am I motivated differently?

_____

_____

How to Present Your Testimony

1. The facilitator will demonstrate a brief testimony that portrays the following points:

• Be joyful. Ask the Lord to give you a pleasant and natural countenance.

• Speak clearly, but in a natural, relaxed tone. Speak loudly enough to be heard.

- Limit your testimony to three minutes in length. This is long enough to say what you need.

- Share your testimony with conviction in the power of the Holy Spirit. Remember that a successful testimony is one communicated in sincerity. Think quality, not quantity.

2. End your testimony with this simple question: "Have you prayed the Sinner's Prayer?"

If the answer is no, ask "Would you like to pray right now?"

Then lead the person in the Sinner's Prayer:

Father, I come to You today to confess my sins and ask You to forgive me of all my sins by the precious blood of Jesus Christ, Your Son, who paid a price I could not pay. Through His obedience unto death, I have been given eternal life. I confess Jesus Christ as my personal Savior and ask Him to be Lord of my life today! Amen.

YOUR WRITTEN TESTIMONY

Ask God to give you wisdom and guidance as you write your testimony:

_____

_____

_____

_____

_____

_____

_____

_____

_____

_____

_____

_____

_____

_____

_____

_____

_____

_____

_____

_____

_____

_____

Be prepared to share your testimony in your small group.

∽ ASSIGNMENT

Please read Chapter Three.

The Holy Spirit and Me:

Walking in Divine Power

"What is the exceeding greatness of His power toward us who believe?"
—EPHESIANS 1:19

PURPOSE STATEMENT: To understand the foundational truth about the incomparable power God has given you to be more than a conqueror. You are an overcomer!

LEARNING OBJECTIVES: This session is designed to help you:

1. Understand water baptism and its significance.
2. Understand your rights as a child of God.
3. Understand what it means to live by faith and receive the Holy Spirit's power in all situations.
4. Understand what you can do to be prepared for spiritual conflict.

SCRIPTURE REFERENCE:

Colossians 1:10–11

"That you may walk worthy of the Lord, fully pleasing Him being fruitful in every good work, and increasing in the knowledge of God; strengthened with all might, according to His glorious power, for all patience and longsuffering with joy."

INTRODUCTION

Answer the two questions below as you begin this session:

Would you like to be obedient to God's Word regarding water baptism? The Lord Himself was baptized: "When He had been baptized, Jesus came up immediately from the water; and behold, the heavens were opened to Him, and He saw the Spirit of God descending like a dove and alighting upon Him" (Matt. 3:16).

_____

Would you like to know how to experience a full, abundant, purposeful, and fruitful life for Christ? You have that opportunity through the power of the Holy Spirit. John the Baptist said, "I indeed baptize you with water unto repentance, but He who is coming after me is mightier than I, whose sandals I am not worthy to carry. He will baptize you with the Holy Spirit and fire" (Matt. 3:11).

_____

What greater promise could Christ have offered to Christians than the assurance of walking daily in the Spirit of Jesus Christ and experiencing an abundant, fruitful life?

WHO I AM AS A CHRISTIAN

Now think about what it means to be a follower of Christ. You are . . .

The Temple of the Holy Spirit:

First Corinthians 6:19: "Or do you not know that your body is the temple of the Holy Spirit who is in you, whom you have from God, and you are not your own?"

Sealed with the "Holy Spirit of promise":

Ephesians 1:13: "In Him you also trusted, after you heard the word of truth, the gospel of your salvation; in whom also, having believed, you were sealed with the Holy Spirit of promise."

Translated into God's Kingdom:

Colossians 1:13: "He has delivered us from the power of darkness and conveyed us into the kingdom of the Son of His love."

Holy and Without Blame Before God:

Ephesians 1:3–4: "Blessed be the God and Father of our Lord Jesus Christ, who has blessed us with every spiritual blessing in the heavenly places in Christ, just as He chose us in Him before the foundation of the world, that we should be holy and without blame before Him in love."

A Joint Heir with Christ Jesus

Romans 8:16–17: "The Spirit Himself bears witness with our spirit that we are children of God, and if children, then heirs—heirs of God and joint heirs with Christ, if indeed we suffer with Him, that we may also be glorified together."

WHO I AM AS A DAUGHTER OF THE KING

I am also a member of God's family. As a daughter of the King I am . . .

A Fellow Citizen with the Saints:
Ephesians 2:19: "Now, therefore, you are no longer strangers and foreigners, but fellow citizens with the saints and members of the household of God."

The Apple of My Father's Eye:
Deuteronomy 32:10: "He found him in a desert land and in the wasteland, a howling wilderness; He encircled him, He instructed him, He kept him as the apple of His eye."

Beloved of God:
Colossians 3:12: "Therefore, as the elect of God, holy and beloved, put on tender mercies, kindness, humility, meekness, longsuffering."

Blessed:
Deuteronomy 28:1–8

"Now it shall come to pass, if you diligently obey the voice of the LORD your God, to observe carefully all His commandments which I command you today, that the LORD your God will set you high above all nations of the earth.

"And all these blessings shall come upon you and overtake you, because you obey the voice of the LORD your God:

"Blessed shall you be in the city, and blessed shall you be in the country.

"Blessed shall be the fruit of your body, the produce of your ground and the increase of your herds, the increase of your cattle and the off-spring of your flocks.

"Blessed shall be your basket and your kneading bowl.

"Blessed shall you be when you come in, and blessed shall you be when you go out.

"The LORD will cause your enemies who rise against you to be defeated before your face; they shall come out against you one way and flee before you seven ways.

"The LORD will command the blessing on you in your storehouses and in all to which you set your hand, and He will bless you in the land which the LORD your God is giving you."

Qualified to Share in Jesus' Inheritance:

Colossians 1:12 "giving thanks to the Father who has qualified us to be partakers of the inheritance of the saints in the light."

SEVEN STEPS TO RECEIVE INFILLING OF THE HOLY SPIRIT

Do you want to receive all that God has for you? If so, ask the Lord to fill you with His Holy Spirit. Read the Scriptures and then take the following seven steps:

Step One: Repentance.

1 John 1:9: "If we confess our sins He is faithful and just to forgive us our sins and to cleanse us from all unrighteousness."

Step Two: Salvation by faith.

Ephesians 2:8–9: "For by grace you have been saved through faith, and that not of yourselves; it is the gift of God, not of works, lest anyone should boast."

Step Three: Be Baptized in Water.

Acts 2:38: "Then Peter said to them, 'Repent, and let every one of you be baptized in the name of Jesus Christ for the remission of sins; and you shall receive the gift of the Holy Spirit."

Step Four: Thirst for Jesus. Have a Passion for God.

John 7:37–38: "On the last day, that great day of the feast, Jesus stood and cried out, saying, 'If anyone thirsts, let him come to Me and drink. He who believes in Me, as the Scripture has said, out of his heart will flow rivers of living water.'"

Step Five: Ask.

Luke 11:13: "If you then, being evil, know how to give good gifts to your children, how much more will your heavenly Father give the Holy Spirit to those who ask Him!"

Step Six: Surrender.

Romans 6:13: "And do not present your members as instruments of unrighteousness to sin, but present yourselves to God as being alive from the dead, and your members as instruments of righteousness to God."

Step Seven: Believe God Is for You and Receive the Holy Spirit.

See John the Baptist's words in Matthew 3:11, Mark 1:8, Luke 3:16, John 1:26 and Acts 1:5.

ᏫᎧ ASSIGNMENT

Please read Chapter Four.

Close in prayer.

Father, I ask that You reveal Yourself to me in a way I have never known before. If there is something about You that I have not experienced, then show me. I ask You to pour Your Holy Spirit into my heart. With this infilling, I ask You to impart in me the passion to witness as Your disciples did on the day of Pentecost. I ask that You help me with my prayer life, lifting me to levels far beyond my natural strength and understanding. When I pray, I want the authority and power of the living God. Guide me, through Your Holy Spirit, in the path You would have me go.

Father, I ask that You pour out into my heart a love so rich that it can only be described as agape love. A love that is so pure its only source can be the throne of the living God. Lord, if there is more of You, then I want to have it. Amen.

Dreams with a Happy Ending:

Setting Goals

"Write the vision and make it plain on tablets."
—HABAKKUK 2:2

PURPOSE STATEMENT: To know the principles of setting godly, measurable, and attainable goals for your life in Christ.

LEARNING OBJECTIVES: This session is designed to help you:
1. Seek the vision of God for your life.
2. Understand the importance of writing this vision down.
3. Understand the process of setting goals to accomplish this vision.
4. Understand how to align your goals with God's will.
5. Learn to wait on the vision.

SCRIPTURE REFERENCE:

Proverbs 16:9

"A man's heart plans his way, but the LORD directs his steps."

THE PROCESS OF GOAL-SETTING

Begin this process by taking two initial steps:

1. List Your Talents and Skills

Don't try to be overly humble here. Honesty is the best policy for accurate goal-setting.

List your skills (a proficiency) in the space below:

_____

_____

List your talents (a natural ability) in the space below:

_____

_____

2. Now Ask This Question: How Can I Use These Skills and Talents in My Life?

For instance, someone who is good in math might want to become a book-keeper, an accountant, or an engineer. Someone who is gifted in hospitality might want to use this gift at church and in her home or in a business such as event planning, hotel management, and entertainment.

SHORT-TERM GOAL-SETTING

In preparation for the goal-setting process in Chapter Five, take a moment now to think about a short-term goal. Write it in the space below:

Goal:

_____

_____

Now think of an obstacle that might keep you from this goal. Write it in the space below:

Obstacle:

_____

_____

Then devise a game plan to counteract this obstacle. Write it in the space below:

Game Plan:

_____

_____

Finally picture what will happen if you achieve this goal. Write that in the space below:

Success:

_____

_____

LONG-TERM GOAL-SETTING

Now also consider one long-term goal. Write it in the space below:

Goal:

_____

_____

Now think of an obstacle that might keep you from this goal. Write it in the space below:

Obstacle:

_____

_____

Then devise a game plan to counteract this obstacle. Write it in the space below:

Game Plan:

_____

_____

Finally picture what will happen if you achieve this goal. Write that in the space below:

Success:

_____

_____

Encourage one another to set goals and pray that each of you will reach your goals.

THE EIGHT-STEP PROCESS OF GOAL-SETTING

Now you are ready to go through the goal-setting process in Chapter Five:

1. Seek God's will.
2. Make time to be with the Lord.
3. Get a vision for your future.
4. Write down your vision and make it plain.
5. Check your goals with the Word of God.
6. Stay focused on your vision; don't give way to a defeated attitude.
7. Make your game plan.

Be ready for success!

∽ ASSIGNMENT

Please read Chapter Five.

Prayer:

Father, You know the plans You have for me, plans to prosper me and not harm me, plans for my future. I was created in Your image for a purpose. You have given me gifts and talents to accomplish Your purpose. Show me these gifts and talents, that I may develop them. Bind my mind to the mind of Christ Jesus, renewing me daily, that I will be conformed to the image of Christ Jesus. According to Your Word, whoever lacks wisdom needs only to ask, and I am asking for wisdom, understanding, and knowledge. Establish my feet on the path You have set before me. Direct my goals as You direct my feet. Father, Your Word is a lamp to my feet and a light to my path. Set my heart and mind on You. Amen.

To God Be the Glory!

Ten Commandments for Women in the Workplace:

Be Diligent in All Things

"In all things showing yourself to be a pattern of good works; in doctrine showing integrity, reverence, incorruptibility."

—TITUS 2:7

PURPOSE STATEMENT: To walk the life of a transformed creature in the workplace, knowing that you are a light drawing others to Christ and a reflection of His love.

LEARNING OBJECTIVES: This session is designed to help you:
1. Understand your position as an ambassador of Christ.
2. Understand how everything you do and say is a witness to the lost around you.

SCRIPTURE REFERENCE:

Psalm 90:17

"And let the beauty of the LORD our God be upon us, and establish the work of our hands for us."

INTRODUCTION

All of God's creation is in the process of working in one way or another. In fact, God Himself worked in the beginning and continues to work today: "For in six days the LORD made the heavens and the earth, the sea and all that is in them, and rested the seventh day" (Ex. 20:11).

WORK

1. The basic definition of work—"physical or mental effort or activity directed toward the production or accomplishment of something"[1]—clearly indicates that work requires effort and action on our part. Work is supposed to yield a positive result, including our personal satisfaction and ultimately God's blessing. We work because we were created to work:

> "You will eat the fruit of your labor; blessings and prosperity will be yours" (Ps. 128:2 NIV).

> "There is nothing better for a man, than that he should eat and drink, and that he should make his soul enjoy good in his labour" (Eccl. 2:24, KJV).

2. Work is a mandate from God, whether in your job or in your home (Ex. 20:9).

3. The benefits of work: "Give her of the fruit of her hands, and let her own works praise her in the gates" (Prov. 31:31).

4. Excellence in work brings us great rewards: God's blessings, a great reputation, a raise in pay or a promotion. Above all, work is pleasing to the Father as

we use every gift He has given us. Work can be glorifying to Him! Scripture says, "And whatever you do, do it heartily, as to the Lord and not to men" (Col. 3:23).

5. We need to work in a right attitude: "Do all things without complaining and disputing, that you may become blameless and harmless, children of God without fault in the midst of a crooked and perverse generation, among whom you shine as lights in the world" (Phil. 2:14–15).

APPLICATION

List four things you can do to be a better example and witness in your workplace or at home.

_____

_____

_____

_____

✌ ASSIGNMENT

Please read Chapter Six.

Close in prayer:

Father, I pray that You will write Your law on my heart. I will meditate on Your law day and night and do according to all that is written. Because of Christ Jesus I am a woman of integrity, and I desire to live this life of integrity. I am the head, not the tail. I am above, not beneath. I know that You will bless whatever I set my hands to. My desire is to become a woman of excellence, that everything I do will testify to Your grace and faithfulness and glorify my Father. In Jesus' name, I pray. Amen.

Women and Their Relationships:

A Godly Heritage

"Fulfill my joy by being like-minded, having the same love, being of one accord, of one mind."

—PHILIPPIANS 2:2

PURPOSE STATEMENT: To learn the importance of how honor and respect invested in others will reap great rewards and blessings.

LEARNING OBJECTIVES: This session is designed to help you:
1. Honor your mother and father; understand the role of the parent/child relationship.
2. Submit to one another in marriage out of reverence for Christ.
3. Understand your role as a single woman.

SCRIPTURE REFERENCES:

Exodus 20:12

   "Honour thy father and thy mother; that thy days may be long upon the land which the LORD thy God giveth thee" (KJV).

Ephesians 5:21–22

"Submitting to one another in the fear of God. Wives, submit to your own husbands, as to the Lord."

Isaiah 54:5

"For your Maker is your husband, The LORD of hosts is His name; And your Redeemer is the Holy One of Israel; He is called the God of the whole earth."

PARENT/CHILD RELATIONSHIPS

1. A Child's Relationship with Parents
Children are instructed to obey their parents.

> "My son, hear the instruction of your father, and do not forsake the law of your mother" (Prov. 1:8).

God promises to reward those children who are obedient with a long and fulfilled life.

> "Honor your father and your mother, as the LORD your God has commanded you, that your days may be long, and that it may be well with you in the land which the LORD your God is giving you" (Deut. 5:16).

As a child, I must reconcile myself to my mother and father if I have not honored their position as instructed by God.

List how you have offended your mother and/or father in the space below:

_____

_____

Repent and ask God to direct you in reconciliation to your parents. Then write a letter to them in the space below:

_____

_____

_____

_____

_____

2. A Parent's Relationship to a Child

As a parent I will instruct my children to obey and honor their father and me as I walk in righteousness. I will strive to train my children without provoking them. Proverbs 22:6 says, "Train up a child in the way he should go, and when he is old he will not depart from it."

List how you have not been a good example to your children in the space below:

_____

_____

_____

_____

_____

List ways you can better train your children to respect their father and you.

_____

_____

_____

_____

_____

3. Our Relationship to God

Deuteronomy 6:5–7

"You shall love the LORD your God with all your heart, with all your soul, and with all your strength. And these words which I command you today shall be in your heart. You shall teach them diligently to your children, and shall talk of them…"

GOD'S WORD ABOUT COURTSHIP AND WOMEN

Single Women

1. Those who are single are cautioned to seek a mate who is a believer: "Do not be unequally yoked together with unbelievers. For what fellowship has righteousness with lawlessness? And what communion has light with darkness" (2 Cor. 6:14).

2. The Word of God promises to give you your heart's desire.

List the character traits that you desire in a husband. Make sure they agree with the Word of God. Copy this list and place it in your Bible. Then wait upon the Lord and His provision.

_____

_____

_____

_____

_____

Now ask the Lord to create in you the characteristics that a godly husband would desire in a wife.

_____

_____

_____

_____

_____

A SINGLE WOMAN'S PRAYER

Lord, I seek You to guide me and direct every step I take. I won't look at others to complete me, because I have You as my Companion, Brother, Father, and Lord. Help me to be complete in You, Lord.

You created me with purpose, and I know Your desire is for me to wait for Your best. Help me to wait on You, Lord. I want Your best. I hereby commit myself to You, to remain pure and set apart until I marry.

I ask You, Father, to prepare the man You created as my husband to receive me as You have received me. I want to have a heart for You, Father, so Your joy will be my strength. In Jesus' name. Amen.

If you are single and have made a decision to remain single, pray this prayer:

Father, as a single woman I acknowledge my place in You and Your role in my life. I know You as my Savior, and I believe in You and Your Word.

The spiritual strength I receive from You enables me to be happy and fulfilled, regardless of my marital status, for You are my Husband, my Provider, my Protector. I desire a passion for Your holiness so that I may experience Your fullness in my life as I seek to know You, love You, and follow Your Word. Thank you, Lord, for completing me! Amen.

MARRIAGE IN A CHRISTIAN'S LIFE

Marriage should be based on a decision directed by the Holy Spirit.

Marriages that are loveless can be saved and restored as we conform to the image of God as women, seeking His face.

God's plan is for husband and wife to be completed in the marriage relationship, walking as one in spirit and truth.

CHARACTERISTICS OF A GODLY WIFE

She loves all others second to Christ Jesus. "But seek first the kingdom of God and His righteousness, and all these things shall be added to you" (Matt. 6:33).

She has an awesome fear of God. "when they observe your chaste conduct accompanied by fear. Do not let your adornment be merely outward—arranging the hair, wearing gold, or putting on fine apparel—rather let it be the hidden person of the heart, with the incorruptible beauty of a gentle and quiet spirit which is very precious in the sight of God" (1 Peter 3:2–4).

She recognizes her husband as the head of the house. "Wives, submit to your own husbands, as to the Lord" (Eph. 5:22).

She prays for her husband and her children. "And this I pray, that your love may abound still more and more in knowledge and all discernment, that you may approve the things that are excellent, that you may be sincere and without offense till the day of Christ" (Phil.1:9–10).

A MARRIED WOMAN'S PRAYER

As a married woman, Lord, I repent. I ask You to forgive me for the unkind and discouraging words I have spoken to my husband. Forgive me for depending on him to make me happy and placing unbearable expectations upon him. You are my joy and my Source. Help me, Lord, to lift up my husband daily in prayer for he who hungers and thirsts after righteousness will be satisfied.

Thank you, Father, for blessing my husband and enlarging his territory. Keep Your hand upon him and keep him from evil that he will cause no harm.

Father, I thank You for the gift of my husband. Help me to show respect and honor to him. He is the priest of my home. I praise You, that he seeks first the kingdom of God and Your righteousness, and that everything will be added to him. I am being conformed daily to the image of Christ Jesus. Let every word I speak honor my husband, that his whole household will be blessed. In Jesus' name, I pray. Amen.

A WOMAN WHO IS MARRIED TO AN UNSAVED HUSBAND

If you are a woman who is married to an unsaved husband, try to fit in with your husband's plans. If your husband refuses to listen when you talk about the Lord, he will be won by your respectful, pure behavior. Your godly life will speak better than any words. Be beautiful inside, in your heart, with the lasting charm of a gentle and quiet spirit that is so precious to God. "But let it be the hidden person of the heart, with the incorruptible beauty of a gentle and quiet spirit, which is very precious in the sight of God" (1 Peter 3:4).

However, if your husband is abusive, neglectful in supplying financial provision for you and your family or has abandoned you, even though you have been a submissive wife and mother, please seek godly counsel and direction.

ONE WAY EVERYDAY

O.W.E.

I spoke of the power of One Way Everyday in my life. Think about your own life as you fill out the O.W.E. form below. If you are not married, think of a family member or close friend who would be blessed with O.W.E.—a parent or a sibling who needs some special love at this time.

1. _____

_____

_____

_____

2. _____

_____

_____

_____

3. _____

_____

_____

_____

ASSIGNMENT

Please read Chapter Seven.

And God Said . . . "Let There Be Sex":

Intimate and Unashamed

"Then God said, 'Let us make man in Our image, according to Our likeness.'"

—GENESIS 1:26

PURPOSE STATEMENT: To accept the truth that you are created in God's image and to understand God's plan for sexuality.

LEARNING OBJECTIVES: This session is designed to help you:

1. To understand God's purpose for sexual purity in your life.
2. To expose the consequences of the world's immoral lifestyle.
3. To reconcile with God and yourself, the scars of your past negative sexual experiences.

SCRIPTURE REFERENCES:

Ephesians 5:3

"But fornication and all uncleanness or covetousness, let it not even be named among you, as is fitting for the saints."

Hebrews 13:4

"Marriage is honorable among all, and the bed undefiled; but fornicators and adulterers God will judge."

INTRODUCTION

Unlike the other topics discussed in our workbook, this lesson will be reviewed by you in the privacy of your home. Dr. Scott Farhart states that every week in his office he sees women who have made the wrong sexual choices. These women represent the world as well as the church. Just like fire can keep us warm and cook our food, it can also scar us permanently and even kill us when it's out of control; sex can be beautiful or destructive.

We address three different groups in our class. First, the unmarried women who ask two questions after hearing about sexually transmitted diseases. Can I be forgiven of my past and, secondly, can I find a godly man?

I encourage them and you to repent of your past and accept God's forgiveness. More importantly, I remind both of you of the importance of forgiving yourselves.

Do not be fearful of the future God has planned for you. There is a godly man who is praying for a woman of God, a King's daughter, to come into his life.

Secondly, I address the women who are in unhappy and unfulfilled marriages. I say, "You are tired of being in a relationship that does not give you what God has ordained for your marriage. Love, affection, intimacy, and respect are all qualities we deserve as godly women. We must allow our Father to work in us so we can be the loving wives we should be, which will release Him to create in our husbands the affectionate spouses we desire.

Finally, I address the women who have been sexually abused; maybe as a child, maybe as an adult, or maybe even by a husband. Many of these women carry the guilt and pain for the rest of their lives. I say to them and to you, "The voice inside you has told you for years that you don't deserve happiness, you are dirty. I want to replace that liar's voice with another voice. This voice says, 'I love you. I care for you. I know what happened to you, for the good or the bad. I've been waiting for you to come for healing so I can give it.' This is the voice of Jesus Christ. For all of these years, He's been waiting for you to come forward to receive healing."

Some of you have been harmed sexually or have made sexual mistakes. I believe that you must put these situations in God's hands and accept His healing. Choose the prayers below that apply to your situation:

PRAYER: FOR THOSE WHO HAVE BEEN VIOLATED

Father, I acknowledge the violation that was committed against me. I place it right now in Jesus Christ's nail-pierced hands. I ask You to give me grace to forgive _____ who violated me. I have been held hostage to this offense and will no longer be held captive.

Your Word says, "If you forgive men their trespasses, Your heavenly Father will also forgive you." What this person did was wrong. It was sin, but I choose no longer to be held in bondage. No weapon formed against me shall prosper, and every tongue that rises up to accuse me, Father, You will deal with. That is my inheritance.

Thank You for Your healing power working in my life right now. Heal my memory, heal my emotions, heal my body by the blood of Jesus Christ. I bind the spirit of rejection that was imparted to me through this violation, and I receive the spirit of adoption extended to me by the cross of Jesus Christ. Restore to me the hope of my salvation and the blessings that come with that hope.

In the name of Jesus, as I forgive _____ *, I pray that he/she will come to the saving knowledge of Jesus Christ and seek Your forgiveness and healing.*

Father, You see me with the robe of righteousness that Your Son purchased on my behalf. You see me as pure and whole. I am completed in You. In Jesus' name. Amen.

PRAYER FOR WOMEN WHO HAVE BEEN PROMISCUOUS

Father, forgive me for I have sinned against You and Your temple. I ask in Jesus' name that You forgive me of all my sins and transgressions. I want to walk in Your fellowship and blessings. I repent of my sins and ask that You renew my mind daily. Create in me a pure heart, Lord. Change me. Mold me into a woman of God. I desire Your righteousness. I consecrate myself to You, Lord, for You are a holy God. In Jesus' name. Amen.

PRAYER FOR MARRIED WOMEN

Father, bless my marriage bed. Let no impurity taint what You have joined together. I thank You for my husband and our sexual union. I pray that neither of us will ever look elsewhere to meet our needs. As a wife help me to remember that it is my ministry to meet my husband's sexual needs. I desire to make myself attractive to him as I would for the King. Lord, help me to let my husband know he is special to me. I desire that he will see Your love for him through me. Amen.

∽ ASSIGNMENT

Please read Chapter Eight.

The Temple of the Lord:

My Body, a Vessel of Honor

"Do you not know that your body is the temple of the Holy Spirit who is in you?"

—I Corinthians 6:19

PURPOSE STATEMENT: To understand God's incredible gift of life and your responsibility as a steward of this gift.

LEARNING OBJECTIVES: This session is designed to help you:
1. Understand the relevance of your body as a temple of the Holy Spirit.
2. Understand moderation and the importance of balance.
3. Distinguish between good and bad habits.

SCRIPTURE REFERENCES:

1 Corinthians 9:27

"But I discipline my body and bring it into subjection, lest, when I have preached to others, I myself should become disqualified."

1 Corinthians 10:31

"Therefore, whether you eat or drink, or whatever you do, do all to the glory of God."

INTRODUCTION

As you begin this session, think about the proclamation below:

My Body Is a Testimony.

"therefore glorify God in your body" (1 Cor. 6:20)

My Body Should Bring Glory to God.

When I take care of my body, I am bringing glory to God.

When I think pure thoughts, I am bringing glory to God.

When I sing praises to God, I am bringing glory to God.

When I pray, I am bringing glory to God.

When I serve, I am bringing glory to God.

When I share Christ, I am bringing glory to God.

My body is His Body, and He should get the glory from it.

THE IMPORTANCE OF HEALTHY WEIGHT

Dr. Don Colbert gave us God's plan for our bodies and how we have unfortunately gotten off course. In this session, we will review some of the facts he presented so they will become a part of our lives.

1. Write some benefits of healthy weight in the space below:

_____

_____

_____

2. Name some of the diseases associated with obesity in the space below:

_____

_____

_____

Are you ready to pledge yourself to natural weight loss if you are overweight?
_____ yes _____no

WHY DIETS FAIL

In the teaching video Dr. Colbert reviewed the different diets many people try. Test your memory against these facts:

1. Give three reasons why fad diets are problematic:

_____

_____

_____

2. List the reasons low-fat diets make you fat:

_____

_____

SUGAR AND CARBOHYDRATES

Dr. Colbert warned against foods that have been altered by man, like sugar and carbohydrates. "We're a nation of sugar addicts," he said.

1. Give the true facts about sugar in the space below:

_____

_____

2. List the sweets you have eaten in the past week:

_____

_____

3. What about carbohydrates? Why are they suspect? List the reasons in the space below:

_____

_____

4. Are all fats bad? _____ yes _____ no. Give the reason for your answer:

_____

5. List the challenges with refined food in the space below:

_____

_____

_____

STEWARDSHIP OF MY BODY, A TEMPLE OF THE LORD

Now think about how you can be a good steward of God's gift. Scripture says, "Therefore if anyone cleanses himself from the latter, he will be a vessel for honor, sanctified and useful for the Master, prepared for every good work" (2 Tim. 2:21).

Take these six steps of good stewardship:

Step One: Repent. Admit that you have not acknowledged your responsibility to maintain your temple. Instead you have used food as a substitute for your relationship with God and/or others. You have also used food to comfort or soothe your hurts and fears. Vow not to do this again.

Step Two: Choose. Make a decision to be healthy! Do this so you will live a healthy, happy, and long life as God intended. "And the LORD said, . . . for he is indeed flesh; yet his days shall be one hundred and twenty years" (Gen. 6:3).

Step Three: Be Accountable. Ask a friend or someone in your group to join you in prayer and talk to each other regularly to encourage one another to be good stewards.

Step Four: Read the Labels. Know what you are putting into your body. Cut back on processed foods such as sugar, white flour, and hydrogenated fats. Better yet, cut them out of your diet. Then watch to see and feel the difference. Read Leviticus, Chapter Eleven.

Step Five: Exercise. You don't have to join a health club, just walk thirty minutes per day–fifteen minutes in one direction and fifteen minutes back. Brisk walking is the ideal exercise for everyone, regardless of age or health.

Step Six: Implement: Take action on what you have learned. "But be doers of the word and not hearers only, deceiving yourselves" (James 1:22).

Remember, God loves you and wants you to enjoy good health! To do so, try an experiment of healthy eating and walking for ten days.

A Ten-Day Experiment

When Daniel was being forced to eat as the Babylonians, he told the king's steward, "Please test your servants for ten days, and let them give us vegetables to eat and water to drink" (Dan. 1:12). Stand up as Daniel did. Test a better nutritional program for ten days.

- Drink more water.
- Eat more vegetables and fruits.
- Increase whole grains.
- Eat meat in moderation.
- Limit or cut out sugar, white flour, and hydrogenated oils.

List the results:
- Did you lose weight?
- Did you lose inches?
- Do you have more energy?
- Do you feel better about yourself?

❧ Assignment

Please read Chapter Nine and follow some of Dr. Don Colbert's suggestions in the days ahead.

Close in prayer:

Lord, I want everything in me to be glorifying to You. Help me to be a good steward of the body You have given me. I confess the times I have complained about my body and spoken against it. I repent and ask Your forgiveness. I know that my body is the temple of Your Holy Spirit who dwells in me.

Father, only You know what is best for me and what is not, so I ask You to instruct me. Take away any confusing and conflicting information I receive from the world and teach me what to eat and what to avoid. I can't do this without You, Lord, for only You know the way You created me.

Help me to be disciplined about what I eat and drink and how I exercise. Enable me to discipline my body and bring it into subjection to Your authority. Help me to fully understand this truth so that I will keep my temple clean and healthy. Help me not to mistreat my body in any way. Teach me to keep this temple pure before You. In Jesus' name, I pray. Amen.

The Favor of God:

A Lesson in Good Stewardship

"From her profits she plants a vineyard."
—PROVERBS 31:16

PURPOSE STATEMENT: To understand the basic principles of the tithe, the seed time, and harvest.

LEARNING OBJECTIVES: This session is designed to help you:
1. Understand the principles of God's economy.
2. Understand tithing.
3. Understand the importance of offerings.
4. Learn to expect your harvest.

SCRIPTURE REFERENCES:

Matthew 6:19–21

"Do not lay up for yourselves treasures on earth, where moth and rust destroy and where thieves break in and steal; but lay up for yourselves treasures in heaven, where neither moth nor rust destroys and where thieves do not break in and steal. For where your treasure is, there your heart will be also."

Matthew 6:24–25

"No one can serve two masters; for either he will hate the one and love the other, or else he will be loyal to the one and despise the other. You cannot serve God and mammon."

INTRODUCTION

Financial resources are for our benefit. They should bless us and not control us. Money is the second most common cause for divorce, therefore there is obvious mismanagement within our marriages and the church body. Let's review some important laws about money.

LAWS OF MONEY

Law One: Truth creates money and lies destroy it.
Law Two: Look at what you have and not at what you had.
Law Three: Do what is right for you before you do what is right for your money.
Law Four: Invest in the known before the unknown.
Law Five: Always remember, money has no power on its own.

During this session you will go through a question-and-answer process to determine how you are spending your money. Let's begin by considering the tithe.

THE IMPORTANCE OF THE TITHE

The tithe is the doorway for the believer into the covenant of blessings. In the Hebrew *maaser* or *maasrah* is translated "tenth" or "tenth part." In Greek *apodekatoo* is translated "give, pay, take, tithe." In both cases these words mean "a payment" or "giving" or "receiving of the tenth."

Our Father provides all of our resources, including our incomes. The tithe is a tenth of our income that is given back to God, which enables Him to move on our behalf in the area of blessing. The Bible records numerous accounts of man tithing to God who is the Creator of everything that exists. The Lord owns everything, and we are simply stewards of what He has entrusted to us. The tithe principle is: He gives to us, we give back to Him, one-tenth of all that He has given to us.

In Malachi 3:10 God makes a promise to us and then challenges us to prove His promise. "'Bring all the tithes into the storehouse, that there may be food in My house, and try Me now in this,' says the LORD of hosts, 'if I will not open for you the windows of heaven and pour out for you such blessing that there will not be room enough to receive it.'" This is the only time in Scripture where God challenges us.

Are you tithing as God requires? Take a test of your stewardship.

A TEST OF YOUR STEWARDSHIP

Think about your own life as you answer the six questions below:

1. *Are you giving at least 10 percent of your earnings to the work of God?*
If not, God says you are using His money and robbing Him. Listen to His words in Malachi 3: "Will a man rob God? Yet you have robbed Me! But you say, 'In what way have we robbed You?' In tithes and offerings" (Mal. 3:8).

2. *Are you giving your tithe to the ministry where you are being fed?*
Our tithe should go to spreading the gospel and the work of our own local church. Offerings above the tithe may be given to the poor and to good works. Additional offerings can also be given to the church's five-fold ministries listed is Ephesians 4:11: apostles, prophets, evangelists, pastors, and teachers.

3. *Are you giving to God first, before paying other bills?*

In Chapter Ten, I mention that even though I tithed, I didn't realize the importance of giving to God first. Scripture says, "Honor the LORD with your possessions, and with the firstfruits of all your increase; so your barns will be filled with plenty, and your vats will overflow with new wine" (Prov. 3:9–10).

4. Are you indifferent to the needs of the poor?

Again Scripture gives us a standard: "He who gives to the poor will not lack, but he who hides his eyes will have many curses" (Prov. 28:27).

5. Are you being wasteful?

After the feeding of the 5,000, Jesus told His disciples, "Gather up the fragments that remain, so that nothing is lost" (John 6:12).

6. Have you committed all your money and material possessions to God?

Jesus said, "For where your treasure is, there your heart will be also" (Luke 12:34).

Now think about your finances and any debt that you may have incurred.

God's Direction about Debt

The Lord is not silent about Christians being in debt. Think about your own life as you answer the three questions below. Note the Scriptures that apply:

1. Are you going into debt for lustful things—wants, instead of needs?

Paul advised the young pastor Timothy: "Now godliness with contentment is great gain. For we brought nothing into this world, and it is certain we can carry nothing out. And having food and clothing, with these we shall be content" (1 Tim. 6:6–9).

2. *Are you too generous in giving to others without paying your own bills?*

Scripture says, "Do not withhold good from those to whom it is due, when it is in the power of your hand to do so" (Prov. 3:27).

3. *Have you paid your debts or made arrangements to do so when you are having difficulties?*

Paul advised the Roman Christians: "Owe no one anything except to love one another, for he who loves another has fulfilled the law" (Rom. 13:8).

Finally consider making some changes in how you handle your money.

DAILY AFFIRMATIONS

To pray over your financial situation, repent first, then vow to become obedient to God's Word. Ask God to show Himself to you and break the bondage of debt over your life. Then use these affirmations on a daily basis until you believe the Scriptures on which they are based:

Monday: "God has not given me a spirit of fear, but of power, and of love, and of a sound mind" (2 Tim. 1:7).

Tuesday: "I honor the LORD with my substance, and with the firstfruits of all my increase: so shall my barns be filled with plenty, and my presses shall burst out with new wine" (Prov. 3:9–10 KJV).

Wednesday   "And God is able to make all grace abound toward you, that you, always having all sufficiency in all things, may have an abundance for every good work" (2 Cor. 9:8).

Thursday   "If you are willing and obedient, you shall eat the good of the land" (Is. 1:19).

Friday   "Give, and it will be given to you: good measure, pressed down, shaken together, and running over will be put into your bosom. For with the same measure that you use, it will be measured back to you" (Luke 6:38).

Saturday: "But this I say: He who sows sparingly will also reap sparingly, and he who sows bountifully will also reap bountifully" (2 Cor. 9:6).

Tithing arises from obedience and God always rewards obedience. It acknowledges God as our true Source. In our obedience, according to Deuteronomy 28:1–14, "blessings will come upon us and overtake us." We must learn to receive what God has for us when we are obedient.

⌒ ASSIGNMENT

Please read Chapter Ten and consider working through the budgeting process there if you do not have a budget.

Close in prayer:
  Lord, Your Word says that those of us who love Your laws will have great

peace and nothing will cause us to stumble. I love Your law, because I know it is there for my benefit. Enable me to live in obedience so that I will not stumble and fall. Help me to obey You so that I can dwell in the confidence and peace of knowing I am living in Your way.

My heart wants to obey You in all things, Lord. If there are steps of obedience I don't understand, I pray You will open my eyes to see the truth and help me to take those steps. Help me to be ever learning about Your ways so I can live in the fullness of Your presence and move into the future You have for me. Put in me a giving heart. I want to joyfully present my tithe and offering to You and know that You will bless me above and beyond what I could think or imagine. Amen.

Hospitality:

An Attitude of the Heart

"As each one has received a gift, minister it to one another, as good stewards of the manifold grace of God."

—I PETER 4:10

PURPOSE STATEMENT: To learn that in serving others in love, you are imitating Christ.

LEARNING OBJECTIVES: This session is designed to help you:
1. Understand the role of hospitality in the Christian's walk.
2. Recognize your role in servanthood.

SCRIPTURE REFERENCES:

Genesis 18:1–8

"Then the LORD appeared to him by the terebinth trees of Mamre, as he was sitting in the tent door in the heat of the day.

So he lifted his eyes and looked, and behold, three men were standing by him; and when he saw them, he ran from the tent door to meet them, and bowed himself to the ground,

And said, 'My Lord, if I have now found favor in Your sight, do not pass on by Your servant.

'Please let a little water be brought, and wash your feet, and rest yourselves under the tree.

'And I will bring a morsel of bread, that you may refresh your hearts. After that you may pass by, inasmuch as you have come to your servant.' They said, 'Do as you have said.'

So Abraham hastened into the tent to Sarah and said, 'Quickly, make ready three measures of fine meal; knead it and make cakes.'

And Abraham ran to the herd, took a tender and good calf, gave it to a young man, and he hastened to prepare it.

So he took butter and milk and the calf which he had prepared, and set it before them; and he stood by them under the tree as they ate."

1 Peter 4:9

"Be hospitable to one another without grumbling."

WHAT DOES HOSPITALITY INVOLVE?

The dictionary definition of the word *hospitality* is "a cordial and generous reception of guests."[1]

As you consider hospitality as being part of your everyday life, answer these four questions and consider the Scripture references:

1. What are the characteristics of true hospitality?

"A new commandment I give to you, that you love one another; as I have loved you, that you also love one another. By this all will know that you are My disciples, if you have love for one another" (John 13:34–35).

_____

_____

2. As genuine hospitality must flow from love for our fellow human beings, what is fulfilled by its exercise?

"Therefore, as the elect of God, holy and beloved, put on tender mercies, kindness, humility, meekness, longsuffering" (Col. 3:12).

_____

3. Is it my duty to be hospitable? _____ yes _____ no

"Do not forget to entertain strangers, for by so doing some have unwittingly entertained angels" (Heb. 13:2).

4. What will be the final reward for hospitality?

"Then the King will say to those on His right hand, 'Come you blessed of My Father, inherit the kingdom prepared for you from the foundation of the world: for I was hungry and you gave Me food; I was thirsty and you gave Me drink; I was a stranger and you took Me in" (Matt. 25:34–35).

_____

APPLICATION

Mention how you can reach out and show hospitality in the next week in the space below:

_____

_____

_____

☙ ASSIGNMENT

Please read Chapter Eleven.

Prayer:

Father, I come to You in a spirit of gratitude. I thank You for the love, mercy, and grace that You extend to me. Help me to think of others before myself and take on the same mind of Christ, who is equal to You, yet took on the character of a servant. Lord, use me to bless others. Help me to be creative in ways to extend hospitality and kindness. Let the love of Jesus Christ shine through my stewardship of giving to others that the needs of the saints are met and a chorus of thanksgiving is given unto You.

Father, I am not my own, my home is not my own, my resources are not my own. Everything I have and all that I am is Yours. Guide me and direct me. Father, You have shown me, O Lord, what is good, and what You require of me: to show kindness and mercy and to walk humbly with You! Create in me a new heart that desires to reach out to others and to say to the stranger, welcome. Father, thank You for an opportunity to be Your hands, Your feet, and Your love to Your children as I humbly serve them. Please accept my actions as a sweet smelling aroma unto Your throne. In Jesus' name. Amen.

Beauty:

A Mirrored Reflection of Christ

*"Let your light so shine before men, that they may see your good works
and glorify your Father in heaven."*

—Matthew 5:16

PURPOSE STATEMENT: To realize that you are a reflection of what is in your heart.

LEARNING OBJECTIVES: This session is designed to help you:
1. Understand that your beauty is in Christ.
2. Understand the role of faith in living out your identity in Christ.
3. Complement your physical body.

SCRIPTURE REFERENCE:
1 Peter 3:3–4

"Do not let your adornment be merely outward—arranging the hair, wearing gold, or putting on fine apparel—rather let it be the hidden person of the heart, with the incorruptible beauty of a gentle and quiet spirit, which is very precious in the sight of God. "

Your Spiritual Beauty

As a beautiful woman of God, you are identified with Christ. You are . . .

Changed. The moment you trusted in Christ, you experienced a change in your identity. You were identified with Christ in His death and resurrection (Gal. 2:20). You became a new creature in Christ (2 Cor. 5:17). Let's look at each of these Scriptures:

Galatians 2:20

"I have been crucified with Christ; it is no longer I who live, but Christ lives in me; and the life which I now live in the flesh I live by faith in the Son of God, who loved me and gave Himself for me."

2 Corinthians 5:17

"Therefore, if anyone is in Christ, he is a new creation; old things have passed away; behold, all things have become new."

Identified with God's Kingdom of light, rather than Satan's kingdom of darkness.

Colossians 1:13

"He has delivered us from the power of darkness and conveyed us into the kingdom of the Son of His love."

Dead to Sin

Romans 6:11

"Likewise you also, reckon yourselves to be dead indeed to sin, but alive to God in Christ Jesus our Lord."

What two things about your new identity in Christ are the most important to you? Why?

_____

_____

_____

In light of your new identity in Christ, consider these four steps to help you walk as a daughter of the King.

FOUR STEPS TO EXPERIENCING THE DAILY REALITY OF YOUR NEW IDENTITY

Step One: Remember the four truths of your identification with Christ.
- You are crucified with Christ.
- You are dead to sin.
- You are united with Him in a new life.
- You have power from Christ to live the Christian life.

Romans 6:3–9

"Or do you not know that as many of us as were baptized into Christ Jesus were baptized into His death? Therefore we were buried with Him through baptism into death, that just as Christ was raised from the dead by the glory of the Father, even so we also should walk in newness of life. For if we have been united together in the likeness of His death, certainly we also shall be in the likeness of His resurrection, knowing this, that our old man was crucified with Him, that the body of sin might be done away with, that we should no longer be slaves of sin. For he who has died has been freed from sin. Now if we died with Christ, we believe that we shall also live with Him, knowing that Christ, having been raised from the dead, dies no more. Death no longer has dominion over Him."

Step Two: Offer yourself to the Lord.

Yield to Jesus' lordship in your life. Submit yourself to His authority.

Romans 6:12–13 -

"Therefore do not let sin reign in your mortal body, that you should obey it in its lusts. And do not present your members as instruments of unrighteousness to sin, but present yourselves to God as being alive from the dead, and your members as instruments of righteousness to God."

Step Three: Choose to obey Christ in the power of the Holy Spirit.

You cannot obey apart from the power of the Holy Spirit. But you must choose to walk by faith in order to walk in His will.

Romans 6:17–18

"But God be thanked that though you were slaves of sin, yet you obeyed from the heart that form of doctrine to which you were delivered. And having been set free from sin, you became slaves of righteousness."

Step Four: Accept that you are beautiful, created in His image, as His vessel for His glory.

Psalm 139:14–18

"I will praise You, for I am fearfully and wonderfully made. Marvelous are Your works, and that my soul knows very well. My frame was not hidden from You, when I was made in secret, and skillfully wrought in the lowest parts of the earth. Your eyes saw my substance, being yet unformed. And in Your book they all were written, the days fashioned for me, when as yet there were none of them. How precious also are Your thoughts to me, O God! How great is the sum of them! If I should count them, they would be more in number than the sand. When I awake, I am still with You."

Now consider your physical beauty as a daughter of the King.

YOUR PHYSICAL BEAUTY

Read the following thoughts.

A Description of Real Beauty:

- For attractive lips, speak words of kindness.
- For lovely eyes, seek out the good in people.
- For a slim figure, share your food with the hungry.
- For beautiful hair, let a child run his or her fingers through it once a day.
- For poise, walk with the knowledge that you'll never walk alone.

The Beauty of a Woman Is . . .

- Not in the clothes she wears, the figure she carries, or the way she combs her hair.
- Not in a facial mole but true beauty in a woman is reflected in her soul. It is the caring she lovingly gives and the passion she shows.
- Must be seen from within her eyes, because that is the doorway to her heart, the place where love resides.
- Only grows with passing years.

Write down your views of yourself and how they contrast with these thoughts:

_____

_____

_____

Now write how you choose to view yourself as a daughter of the King:

_____

_____

_____

_____

∽ ASSIGNMENT

Please read Chapter Twelve.

Close in prayer.

Lord, I want to be changed, and I pray those changes begin today. I know I can't change myself in any way that is significant or lasting, but by the transforming power of Your Holy Spirit, all things are possible. Transform me into Your likeness. Soften my heart where it has become hard. Make me fresh where I have become stale. Lead me and instruct me where I have become unteachable. Make me faithful, giving, and obedient the way Jesus was. Where I am resistant to change, help me to trust Your work in my life. Make me much more like Christ so that when people see me they will want to know You better. Help me to see myself as beautiful as You see me. In Jesus' name. Amen.

The Favor of God:

Walking in Divine Blessings

"For You O Lord, will bless the righteous; with favor You will surround him as with a shield."

—Psalm 5:12

PURPOSE STATEMENT: To learn to walk in God's favor in every situation and circumstance of your life.

LEARNING OBJECTIVES: This session is designed to help you:
1. Understand God's plan for your life.
2. Understand how to receive God's favor in your life.
3. Know the difference between your will and God's will for your life.

SCRIPTURE REFERENCE:
Proverbs 8:32–35

"Now therefore, listen to me, my children, for blessed are those who keep my ways. Hear instruction and be wise, and do not disdain it. Blessed is the man who listens to me, watching daily at my gates, waiting at the posts of my doors. For whoever finds me finds life, and obtains favor from the LORD."

THE PROCLAMATION OF FAVOR

From the beginning of our journey we have been making proclamations over our lives and the lives of our loved ones. We are about to embark on a new road in the journey to becoming a woman of God that will lead us into His favor. In Psalm 5 King David said, "But let all those rejoice who put their trust in You; let them ever shout for joy, because You defend them. Let those also who love Your name be joyful in You. For You, O LORD, will bless the righteous; with favor You will surround him as with a shield" (vv. 11–12).

GOD'S UNMERITED FAVOR

Take a walk with me through the pages of the Old Testament and see how God's favor is pervasive for His children. God's favor promises . . .

1. Salvation, prosperity, and joy

Psalm 106:4–5
"Remember me, O LORD, with the favor You have toward Your people. Oh, visit me with Your salvation, that I may see the benefit of Your chosen ones, that I may rejoice in the gladness of Your nation, that I may glory with Your inheritance."

2. Supernatural increase and promotion

Genesis 39:21

"But the LORD was with Joseph and showed him mercy, and He gave him favor in the sight of the keeper of the prison."

3. Restoration of everything the enemy has stolen from you

Exodus 3:21

"And I will give this people favor in the sight of the Egyptians; and it shall be, when you go, that you shall not go empty-handed."

4. Honor in the midst of your adversaries

Exodus 11:3

"And the LORD gave the people favor in the sight of the Egyptians. Moreover the man Moses was very great in the land of Egypt, in the sight of Pharaoh's servants and in the sight of the people."

5. Increased assets

Deuteronomy 33:23

"And of Naphtali he said: 'O Naphtali, satisfied with favor, and full of the blessing of the LORD, possess the west and the south.'"

6. Great victories in the midst of impossible odds

2 Chronicles 20:15, 29

"And he said, 'Listen, all you of Judah and you inhabitants of Jerusalem, and you, King Jehoshaphat! Thus says the LORD to you: 'Do not be afraid nor dismayed because of this great multitude, for the battle is not yours, but God's.' . . .

"And the fear of God was on all the kingdoms of those countries when they heard that the LORD had fought against the enemies of Israel."

7. Recognition in the midst of many

1 Samuel 16:22

"Then Saul sent to Jesse, saying 'Please let David stand before me, for he has found favor in my sight.'"

8. Prominence and preferential treatment.

Esther 2:17

"The king loved Esther more than all the other women, and she obtained grace and favor in his sight more than all the virgins; so he set the royal crown upon her head and made her queen instead of Vashti."

9. Petitions granted even by ungodly authority

Esther 5:8

"If I have found favor in the sight of the king, and if it pleases the king to grant my petition and fulfill my request, then let the king and Haman come to the banquet which I will prepare for them, and tomorrow I will do as the king has said."

10. Policies, rules, regulations, and laws changed for your behalf

Esther 8:5

"If it pleases the king, and if I have found favor in his sight and the thing seems right to the king and I am pleasing in his eyes, let it be written to revoke the letters devised by Haman, the son of Hammedatha the Agagite, which he wrote to annihilate the Jews who are in all the king's provinces."

11. Territory gained for your behalf through God's intervention

Psalm 44:3

"For they did not gain possession of the land by their own sword, nor did their own arm save them; but it was Your right hand, Your arm, and the light of Your countenance, because You favored them."

We have heard the Word of the Lord. We must believe the Word of the Lord for our lives. He wants His daughters to prosper in every way. He extends His favor to us; all we must do is ask, obey, and receive.

Let us proclaim the favor of the Lord over our lives:

> *In the name of Jesus, I am the righteousness of God; therefore I am enti-tled to covenant kindness and favor. The favor of God is among the right-eous. His favor surrounds the righteous; therefore, it surrounds me. Everywhere I go, everything I do, I expect the favor of God to be in man-ifestation. Never again will I be without the favor of God.*
>
> *Satan, my days in Lodebar cease today. I am leaving that place of lack and want. I am going from the pit to the palace because the favor of God is on me. God's favor rests richly on me. God's favor profusely abounds in me, and I am part of the generation that will experience the favor of God, immeasurable, limitless, and surpassing.*
>
> *Therefore, God's favor produces in my life supernatural increase, pro-motion, prominence, preferential treatment, restoration, honor, increased assets, great victories, recognition, petitions granted, policies and rules changed on my behalf, and battles won that I don't have to fight. The favor*

of God is upon me, His favor goes before me, and therefore my life will
never be the same again. Amen.

We have just proclaimed something we never thought possible over our lives.
It is time we begin to live in the inheritance our heavenly Father has so freely given
us. The Word of God says that He has never seen the righteous forsaken or their
seed begging for bread (Ps. 37:25). The Word says that God gives us the power to
get wealth (Deut. 8:18). Yet we continue to live outside of our inheritance.

We are daughters of the King. We must begin to believe that we are entitled
to His provision. We must begin to think like daughters of the King. And finally,
we must being to live like daughters of the King.

ᴄᴏ Assignment

Please read Chapter Thirteen to see how God has favored some people in the
ways mentioned in this chapter.

Prayer and Fasting:

Knowing God's Will

"Go, gather all the Jews who are present in Shushan, and fast for me; neither eat nor drink for three days, night or day. My maids and I will fast likewise. And so I will go to the king."

—ESTHER 4:16

PURPOSE STATEMENT: To gain an understanding of the breakthrough and power that comes through personal prayer and fasting.

LEARNING OBJECTIVES: This session is designed to help you to:
1. Understand prayer and fasting.
2. Learn how to pray and fast.
3. Anticipate God's answers.

SCRIPTURE REFERENCES:

Philippians 4:6–7

"Be anxious for nothing, but in everything by prayer and supplication, with thanksgiving, let your requests be made known to God; and the peace of God, which surpasses all understanding, will guard your hearts and minds through Christ Jesus."

Daniel 9:3–4

"Then I set my face toward the Lord God to make request by prayer and supplications, with fasting, sackcloth, and ashes. And I prayed to the LORD my God, and made confession, and said, 'O Lord, great and awesome God, who keeps His covenant and mercy with those who love Him, and with those who keep His commandments.'"

Matthew 6:16–18

"Moreover, when you fast, do not be like the hypocrites, with a sad countenance. For they disfigure their faces that they may appear to men to be fasting. Assuredly, I say to you, they have their reward. But you, when you fast, anoint your head and wash your face, so that you do not appear to men to be fasting, but to your Father who is in the secret place; and your Father who sees in secret will reward you openly."

WHY IS PRAYER IMPORTANT?

Prayer is personal communication with God, which involves listening to God as He speaks to us through His Word.

1. Read Acts 4:23–31, then answer the question: What does this Scripture teach us about prayer?

Acts 4:23–31

And being let go, they went to their own companions and reported all that the chief priests and elders had said to them.

So when they heard that, they raised their voice to God with one accord and said, "Lord, You are God, who made heaven and earth and the sea, and all that is in them, who by the mouth of Your servant David have said:

'Why did the nations rage,
And the people plot vain things?
The kings of the earth took their stand,
And the rulers were gathered together
Against the LORD and against His Christ.'

For truly against Your holy Servant Jesus, whom You anointed, both Herod and Pontius Pilate, with the Gentiles and the people of Israel, were gathered together to do whatever Your hand and Your purpose determined before to be done.

"Now, Lord, look on their threats, and grant to Your servants that with all boldness they may speak Your word, by stretching out Your hand to heal, and that signs and wonders may be done through the name of Your holy Servant Jesus."

And when they had prayed, the place where they were assembled together was shaken; and they were all filled with the Holy Spirit, and they spoke the word of God with boldness.

This Scripture teaches us the following things about prayer:

1. To call on the name of God and acknowledge His greatness.
2. To place our petition before the Lord.
3. To receive by faith God's answer.

How to Pray

Prayer involves our whole being. We pray to the Father in the name and authority of Jesus Christ, His Son, and through the ministry of the Holy Spirit. Jesus said, "You did not choose Me, but I chose you and appointed you that you should go and bear fruit, and that your fruit should remain, that whatever you ask the Father in My name He may give you" (John 15:16).

There are five different ways to pray:

1. Worshiping, praising, and thanking (Ps. 118:1–9).

2. Individual prayer, crying out loud to the Lord or in silent prayer (Ps. 27:7–8).

3. Corporate prayer in a large or small group (Esther 4:16).

4. Praying the Scriptures, the Word of God (Ps. 119:11–12).

5. Praying in your heavenly language (Rom. 8:26–27).

Exercise your time of waiting before the Lord as in Isaiah 40:31.

Now that you have looked at why prayer is so important and the ways you can pray, set a personal appointment with your King for prayer.

PERSONAL APPLICATION OF PRAYER

A format for your personal prayers could go like this:

1. *Repentance*
Matthew 6:12: "And forgive us our debts as we forgive our debtors."

2. *Thank God, worship Him, praise Him*
Psalm 100:4:"Enter into His gates with thanksgiving, and into His courts with praise. Be thankful to Him, and bless His name."

3. *Pray for the peace of Jerusalem/Israel*
Psalm 122:6: "Pray for the peace of Jerusalem: 'May they prosper who love you.'"

4. *Pray for those in authority and in government*
1 Timothy 2:1–2: "Therefore I exhort first of all that supplications, prayers, intercessions, and giving of thanks be made for all men, for kings and all who are in authority, that we may lead a quiet and peaceable life in all godliness and reverence."

5. *Personal Petitions*

Ephesians 6:18–19: "praying always with all prayer and supplication in the Spirit, being watchful to this end with all perseverance and supplication for all the saints—and for me, that utterance may be given to me, that I may open my mouth boldly to make known the mystery of the gospel."

6. *End your prayer time as you began, with thanksgiving and praise*

Psalms 146:1–10: "Praise the LORD! Praise the LORD, O my soul! While I live I will praise the LORD; I will sing praises to my God while I have my being.

Do not put your trust in princes, nor in a son of man, in whom there is no help. His spirit departs, he returns to his earth; in that very day his plans perish.

Happy is he who has the God of Jacob for his help, whose hope is in the LORD his God, who made heaven and earth, the sea, and all that is in them; who keeps truth forever, who executes justice for the oppressed, who gives food to the hungry. The LORD gives freedom to the prisoners.

The LORD opens the eyes of the blind; the LORD raises those who are bowed down; the LORD loves the righteous. The LORD watches over the strangers; He relieves the fatherless and widow; but the way of the wicked He turns upside down.

The LORD shall reign forever—Your God, O Zion, to all generations.

Praise the LORD!"

From these Scriptures you can see that as a King's daughter we must pray to know God's will and walk in His Spirit.

KNOWING THE WILL OF GOD THROUGH PRAYER AND FASTING

Fasting is the act of laying aside food, entertainment, routines, or other worldly activities to focus on the Lord and His Word. Fasting brings intimacy with God, our Father, and breakthroughs in our spiritual and everyday life.

The Lord tells us in Matthew 6:16–18 that when we fast, we are to do so unto the Lord. Jesus gives us a mandate to fast, not a suggestion:

"Moreover, **when you fast**, do not be like the hypocrites, with a sad countenance. For they disfigure their faces that they may appear to men to be fasting. Assuredly, I say to you, they have their reward.

"But you, when you fast, anoint your head and wash your face, so that you do not appear to men to be fasting, but to your Father who is in the secret place; and your Father who sees in secret will reward you openly."

Let's look at some people in the Bible who combined prayer with fasting.

EXAMPLES OF BIBLICAL FASTING

Aside from Esther, the people in the Bible who combined prayer with fasting are Moses, Nehemiah, Daniel, and, of course, Jesus, just to name a few.

Moses: Deuteronomy 9:25–29

"Thus I prostrated myself before the LORD; forty days and forty nights I kept prostrating myself, because the LORD had said He would destroy you.

"Therefore I prayed to the LORD, and said, 'O Lord GOD, do not destroy Your people and Your inheritance whom You have redeemed through Your greatness, whom You have brought out of Egypt with a mighty hand.

'Remember Your servants, Abraham, Isaac, and Jacob; do not look on the stubbornness of this people, or on their wickedness or their sin, lest the land from which You brought us should say, "Because the LORD was not able to bring them to the land which He promised them, and because He hated them, He has brought them out to kill them in the wilderness."

'Yet they are Your people and Your inheritance, whom You brought out by Your mighty power and by Your outstretched arm.'

Ezra: Ezra 10:6

"Then Ezra rose up from before the house of God, and went into the chamber of Jehohanan the son of Eliashib; and when he came there, he ate no bread and drank no water, for he mourned because of the guilt of those from captivity."

Nehemiah: Nehemiah 1:4

"So it was, when I heard these words, that I sat down and wept, and mourned for many days; I was fasting and praying before the God of heaven."

Daniel: Daniel 9:3

"Then I set my face toward the Lord God to make request by prayer and supplications, with fasting, sackcloth, and ashes."

Jesus: Matthew 4:2

"And when He had fasted forty days and forty nights, afterward He was hungry."

Four Biblical Reasons for Fasting:

1. *We receive spiritual cleansing and our spiritual eyes are opened*

> "Is this not the fast that I have chosen:
> To loose the bonds of wickedness,
> To undo the heavy burdens,
> To let the oppressed go free,
> And that you break every yoke?" (Isaiah 58:6)

2. *Fasting loosens the bands of wickedness*

When Jesus discussed the keys to the kingdom, He told us to bind and loose. He said, "And I will give you the keys of the kingdom of heaven, and whatever you bind on earth will be bound in heaven, and whatever you loose on earth will be loosed in heaven" (Matt. 16:19). When we fast, we loose the bands of wickedness, undo heavy burdens, set the oppressed free, and break every yoke of the enemy. Fasting is an important key to victory over hard situations that do not seem to respond to normal prayer.

3. Fasting builds our faith

This is what Jesus meant when He answered the disciples question about why they were not able to cast a demon out of a child. He said, "However, this kind does not go out except by prayer and fasting" (Matt. 17:21). The Lord was telling His disciples, "If you want your faith to be strong enough to cast out demons, you must fast and pray."

4. Fasting makes it easier for us to hear the voice of the Lord

We find an account of this in Acts 13:2–3:

"As they ministered to the Lord and fasted, the Holy Spirit said, 'Now separate to Me Barnabas and Saul for the work to which I have called them.' Then, having fasted and prayed, and laid hands on them, they sent them away."

If you are considering a fast, I suggest you follow this process.

THE PROCESS OF FASTING

Step One: *Check Your Motives.*

Before you fast, you need to check your motives for fasting. Are they selfish? If so, the Lord will not accept your fast.

Psalm 51:10

"Create in me a clean heart, O God, and renew a steadfast spirit within me."

Step Two: *Repent and Confess Your Sins. Ask for forgiveness.*
2 Corinthians 7:9–10

"Now I rejoice, not that you were made sorry, but that your sorrow led to repentance. For you were made sorry in a godly manner, that you might suffer loss from us in nothing. For godly sorrow produces repentance leading to salvation, not to be regretted; but the sorrow of the world produces death."

Step Three: *Choose How You Will Fast.*
Isaiah 58:5

"Is it a fast that I have chosen, a day for a man to afflict his soul? Is it to bow down his head like a bulrush, and to spread out sackcloth and ashes? Would you call this a fast, and an acceptable day to the LORD?"

COMMON FORMS OF FASTING:

1. Partial Fast. Abstinence from certain foods (for instance no meat or sweets).
2. Juice Fast. Fruit and vegetable juices only.
3. Normal Fast. No food, water only.
4. Total Fast. Absolutely no food or water.

(Caution: The total fast should not be undertaken for over three days and only if you have a clear directive from the Lord and are in good health. If you are considering an extended fast, you should seek competent medical supervision of someone familiar with fasting. This is especially true if you are taking any medications.)

There is no assignment for this lesson.

Prayer:

> *Lord, Your Word says that those of us who love Your law will have great peace and nothing will cause us to stumble. I love Your law because I know*

it is good and it is there for my benefit. Enable me to live in obedience in each part of life so that I will not stumble and fall. Help me to obey You so that I can dwell in the confidence and peace of knowing I am living according to Your will.

My heart wants to obey You in all things, Lord, even in fasting and prayer. If there are steps of obedience I need to take that I don't understand, I pray You would open my eyes to see the truth and help me to take those steps. I know I can't do all things right without Your help, so I ask that You would enable me to live in obedience to Your ways. Show me the fast I should take. "With my whole heart I have sought You; Oh, let me not wander from Your commandments!" Help me to be ever learning about Your ways so I can live in the fullness of Your presence and move into all You have for me. Amen.

Notes

Part One
Chapter One

1. J. Vernon McGee, *Thru the Bible with J. Vernon McGee*, Vol. II (Nashville: Thomas Nelson Publishers, 1983), 545.

2. Ibid., 553.

3. Ibid., 546.

Chapter Two

1. Kim Alexis, *A Model for a Better Future* (Nashville: Thomas Nelson Publishers, 1998*)*, 2.

2. Ibid, 7.

3. Ibid, 12.

4. Ibid, 61.

5. Ibid, 61–62.

Chapter Three

1. Leighton Ford, *The Power of Story* (Colorado Springs: Navpress Publishing Group, 1994), 10.

2. Ibid.,

3. Ibid., 11.

4. Ibid., 52.

5. Ibid., 73

6. Ibid., 86–87.

7. Ibid., 122.

8. Ibid., 127.

9. Ibid., 128.

10. Ibid., 153.

Chapter Four

1. J. Vernon McGee, *Thru the Bible with J. Vernon McGee*, Vol. IV (Nashville: Thomas Nelson Publishers, 1983) 582–583.

2. Ibid., 583.

3. Ibid., 474.

Chapter Five

1. *The American Heritage Dictionary* (Boston: Houghton Mifflin Company, 1976), 1351.

2. John Ashcroft, *On My Honor* (Nashville: Thomas Nelson Publishers, 1998), 26–27.
3. Ibid., 195.
4. Ibid., 196–197.

CHAPTER SIX
1. *The American Heritage Dictionary,* 1390.

CHAPTER SEVEN
1. John Trent and Gary Smalley, *The Blessing* (Nashville: Thomas Nelson Publishers, 1986), 24.
2. Ibid., 24.
3. Ibid., 25.
4. Ibid., 26.
5. Ibid., 28.
6. *The American Heritage Dictionary,* 988.
7. Ibid., 988
8. Ibid., 28

CHAPTER EIGHT
1. SexualHealth Update, Summer 1999, Vol. 7, #2, p. 1.
2. Ibid.
3. Corey L. Wald. A Genital Herpes. In: Holmes KK, Mardh PA, Sparling PF et al eds. Sexually Transmitted Diseases. Third ed. New York, NT: McGraw Hill, Co; 1999:285–313, quoted in Sexual Health Update, Spring 2001, Vol. 9, #1, p. 1.
4. Pertel PE. Spear PG. Biology of herpes viruses. In: Holmes KK, Mardh PA, Sparling PF et al eds. Sexually Transmitted Diseases. Third ed. New York, NT: McGraw Hill, Co; 1999:269–284, quoted in Sexual Health Update, Spring 2001, Vol. 9, #1, p. 1.
5. Ibid.,
6. Benedetti J, Corey I., Ashley R. Recurrence rates in genital herpes after symptomatic first-episode infection. *Ann Intern Med.* 1991; 121:847–854. And Benedetti JK, Zeh J. Corey I. Clinical reactivation of genital herpes simplex virus infection decreases in frequency over time. *Ann Intern Med.* 1999; 131:14–20.

CHAPTER TEN
1. Ron Blue, *Master Your Money Workbook* (Nashville: Thomas Nelson Publishers, 1993), 23.

CHAPTER ELEVEN
1. Luis Jacobs, *The Jewish Religion: A Companion* (Oxford: Oxford University Press, 1995), 254.
2. J. Vernon McGee, *Thru the Bible with J. Vernon McGee,* Vol. IV (Nashville: Thomas Nelson Publishers, 1983), 294.

3. Karen Mains, *Open Heart, Open Home* (Elgin, IL: David C. Cook, 1976), 19.

4. Ibid., 20.

5. Ibid., 25.

6. David Lowenstein, as quoted in Lee Stratton, "Dining Together, Once a Family Mainstay, Now Is Fading Practice," *The Columbus Dispatch*, November 21, 1999.

7. Joy Stuart, *The Gift of Cooking with Joy* (Charlotte, North Carolina: Forest Hill Association, 2005), 6.

8. If you are interested in starting a Joy of Cooking class in your church, you may purchase the book on www.foresthillbookstore.org or call 704-716-9633.

CHAPTER TWELVE

1. Susan Wales, *The Art of Romantic Living* (Nashville: Thomas Nelson Publishers, 2002), 239.

2. Ibid., 240–241.

3. Ibid., 247–250.

4. Dr. Don Colbert, *What Would Jesus Eat?* (Nashville: Thomas Nelson Publishers, 2002), 34.

5. Ibid., 39.

6. Ibid., 70.

7. Ibid., 108.

8. Ibid., 165.

9. Ibid., xv.

CHAPTER THIRTEEN

1. J. Vernon McGee, *Thru the Bible with J. Vernon McGee*, Vol. 1 (Nashville: Thomas Nelson Publishers, 1983), 159.

2. Ibid., 161.

PART TWO
LESSON ELEVEN

1. *The American Heritage Dictionary*, 624.

About the Author

DIANA CASTRO HAGEE is the wife of Dr. John C. Hagee, founder and Senior Pastor of Cornerstone Church in San Antonio, Texas, a non-denominational evangelical church with more than 17,000 active members. Together, Pastor Hagee and Diana lead the church and John Hagee Television Ministries and have founded Cornerstone Christian Schools.

Diana Hagee is the author of a cookbook, *Not by Bread Alone,* a guide to creative ministry through food, and *The King's Daughter:* Becoming the Woman God Created You to Be, which received the Third Annual Retailers Choice Award. Diana and her husband have coauthored a book, *What Every Man Wants in a Woman, What Every Woman Wants in a Man.*

Diana serves as Chief of Staff for the John Hagee Ministries television program. She is also Special Events Coordinator and leader of the Women's Ministries at Cornerstone Church. Included among these ministries are Becoming a Woman of God Seminars, the Mother Daughter Banquet, Moms2Moms (a ministry to single moms and their families), MOPS (Mothers of Preschoolers), and Women's Bible Studies and Retreats.

John Hagee Ministries Television telecasts Pastor John Hagee's national radio and television ministry, which is carried in America on 120 full power television stations, 110 radio stations, and three networks and can be seen weekly in 92,031,000 homes. John Hagee Ministries also airs from coast to coast in Canada in prime time on the Vision Network. The ministry is expanding into Europe, Africa, and third world nations.

Diana was presented the prestigious *Lion of Judah* award by the Jewish Federation of Greater Houston for joining her husband in rescuing thousands of Jews from the former Soviet Union, Ethiopia, and other nations of the world and bringing them to Israel. This award signifies a symbol of commitment and solidarity between Christians and Jews on behalf of Jerusalem and the state of Israel. Above all, Diana states that her main job description is to stand by her husband as they lead the beloved church God has given them to pastor: Cornerstone.

Pastor John and Diana Hagee are blessed with five children and three granddaughters.

King's Daughter Resources

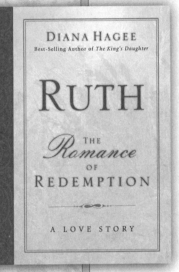

Coming in the fall of 2005 . . .

RUTH
THE ROMANCE OF REDEMPTION
The third book in the King's Daughter series

Diana Hagee challenges women to see the power of Christ's love more clearly as they read of the kinsman redeemer's love for Ruth. This all-encompassing love can both bless us and change our attitudes, our relationships, and our decision-making. Diana challenges us to look for God's hand in each moment. There are no coincidences, she says, just divine appointments.

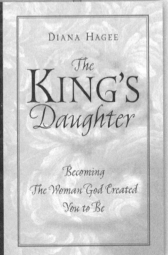

Now available

The KING'S Daughter
BECOMING THE WOMAN GOD CREATED YOU TO BE

In the same way that Mordecai challenged Esther to embrace the divine purpose God had placed before her, *The King's Daughter* challenges each woman to find and take hold of her Father's vision of who she is and what He has called her to do. A Facilitator's Appendix is included at the end of the book so small groups can work through this twelve-week journey together. This book is the first book in the King's Daughter series.

These books are available at Christian bookstores throughout the country or through the Thomas Nelson website: www.thomasnelson.com.

The following products complement the King's Daughter/ Becoming a Woman of God curriculum:

TWELVE MULTIMEDIA SESSIONS ON CD/DVD

Twelve videos of Diana Hagee and guest speakers teaching on the aspects of becoming a woman of God: self-esteem, evangelization, the Holy Spirit, goal-setting, work, relationships, sexuality, stewardship, hospitality, and beauty. These videos compliment either *The King's Daughter Workbook* or *The King's Daughter* sessions.

THE KING'S DAUGHTER FACILITATOR'S HANDBOOK

The guide for discussion leaders and teaching and administrative leaders for both *The King's Daughter* and *The King's Daughter Workbook* curriculum. This handbook and these two books can form either a six-month curriculum or be split into two separate three-month sessions.

INTIMATE AND UNASHAMED BY DR. SCOTT FARHART

In this book Dr. Farhart, one of the guest speakers in the Woman of God curriculum, gives straight answers to questions about sexual issues. This no-nonsense book is a safe resource for accurate medical information based upon godly principles.

THE PRAYER BOX NECKLACE

This necklace symbolizes the women of Esther. The sides of the prayer box have myrtle, the Hebrew letters of Esther's name, the crown, and the cross. The top of the box can be removed to insert a prayer or a blessing. The prayer box necklace can be used as a gift for women who complete the course.

THE PROCLAMATION BOOK OF PRAYERS

Women of God often use prayers of proclamation to foresee a future in which a person or a loved one will be healed or changed. Proclamations of restoration, reconciliation, favor, finances, healthy relationships, servanthood, faith, discernment, blessing, and protection are included in this book.

Myrrh Anointing Oil

When Diana Hagee chose twenty-four women to serve as members of the Women of Esther she gave the women two gifts, one of which was a bottle of anointing oil. She knew they would use this gift often as they served the body of Christ.

Ten Graduation Certificates

Certificates for women who complete a twelve-week woman of God seminar.

Promotional Material CD

A CD with a church bulletin ad and newspaper ads in several sizes, 8.5 x 11 four-color flyers, and 11 x 17 four-color posters. Also editable PDFs that can be used on a PC or Mac so each organization can personalize these items with their specific logistical information.

The King's Daughter Apron and Bag

The other gift that Diana Hagee gave the Women of Esther was an apron. She told them, "God tells us in His Word that the greatest of all will be the servant of all. Your apron should be the dirtiest in the house. In fact every stain on your apron should tell a story. 'This is the pasta party we had for a girlfriend who had a baby' or 'This is the enchilada sauce we prepared when we helped a friend's family after a beloved member died.'"

The King's Daughter Package for Group Programs

This starter kit includes all of the above products, which are in the Woman of God curriculum.

∽

These materials can be purchased through www.johnhagee.net or by calling 1-800-854-9899. In Canada call 1-416-447-4000.